A HEART
FOR
HEALING

'Donald Werner is a very gifted teacher
who writes out of a wise pastoral heart.
Although both Donald and his wife Irene
have experienced real suffering in their
family and are indebted to the medical
profession, this in no way deters him from
an effective ministry of healing. He writes
in a most wholesome and biblical manner,
with engaging illustration.

'I warmly commend this gentle and
refreshing book and pray it will stir the
church to press on in the healing ministry.'

Bishop David Pytches

A HEART FOR HEALING

DONALD K. WERNER

HIGHLAND BOOKS

Biblical quotations are from the New International Version
© International Bible Society 1973, 1978, 1984, unless
otherwise stated

ISBN 0 946616 61 2

Cover design: Diane Drummond

Printed in Great Britain for
HIGHLAND BOOKS
Broadway House, The Broadway,
Crowborough, East Sussex TN6 1HQ
by Richard Clay Ltd, Bungay, Suffolk
Typeset by Rowland Phototypesetting Ltd,
Bury St Edmunds, Suffolk

To my wife
IRENE
partner in
love, life and truth

CONTENTS

INTRODUCTION

'Keep on walking, the hip is all right.' These were the words spoken by a very firm but kindly nurse to a middle-aged man in hospital. He had just had a hip replacement operation which had been wonderfully successful; yet to look at the man's face you would not have come to that conclusion. He was in agony. He tentatively started walking but every time he put weight on his new hip his face would twist with pain. 'Keep on walking, the hip is all right,' seemed to be a most insensitive way of speaking to him, but the nurse was telling him the truth whether he could receive it or not. He had been so used to suffering agony for years with his old hip that his brain, his nervous system, his mind, his emotions were all telling him a lie about the condition of his hip.

His future freedom to walk normally depended upon his facing this new truth. If the nurse had pretended that the hip operation had been a failure in order to help the man understand how he was feeling, he would have sunk back into despair and might never have walked again. As it was, arm in arm with the nurse, he was firmly escorted around the tables in the centre of the ward. Then he sat down to recover. The nurse was not denying that he was feeling pain but rather encouraging him to have faith in the success of his hip operation despite his feelings. He had to practise putting faith in a new reality – the plastic hip!

I visited that man a week later. He was beginning to live a new life – walking normally and without pain. The truth about his new hip had sunk in; and that truth had made him free.

To be a healthy Christian we need to know the truth about ourselves and stop believing lies. We are new creations – the old has passed away and the new has come. The father of lies wants us to believe lies; to believe, for example, that the 'operation' which the Great Physician performed on us through his cross was less than a total success.

This book is intended to help us – as the nurse helped the man – to face the new truth about ourselves. The starting point must be what the God of Truth says about us, and not what we feel or think or how we would analyse our condition. If we start with our feelings then we can easily be diverted from the truth and go hobbling about all our lives suffering from an overdose of introversion. As we realise what the Lord has done for us and his desire to heal us, we can hear him say: 'You shall know the truth and the truth shall set you free.'

Chapter 1

GOD'S HEART FOR HEALING

Does God really want to heal *us*?

It is very important that we give an unambiguous reply to that question. My own personal testimony to healing illustrates this point.

I used to have hay fever very badly indeed. Although it's my nature to fight ailments away, sometimes it was impossible. When I was a university chaplain in Bristol there were days in which I had to draw the curtains of my room and lie down, totally exhausted by hay fever. Life during the summer months was like continually breathing in pepper.

Each summer I went to the GP, who gave me tablets that had the effect of toning everything down and making me feel drowsy. I had been given several series of injections for hay fever but they didn't help. During all the time I was suffering I never doubted God's power to heal.

One summer, when the pollen count was at its highest, I gave a talk on God's power to heal. I was not a very good visual aid for my talk, as I had to blow my nose every five to ten minutes! A student, Brian, was sitting next to me in the meeting room. He had eczema so badly that his hands were covered with polythene bags saturated with ointment; he also had mild hay fever and asthma and, to make things more critical, his university exams were the following week. I had just finished the Bible study on healing, when Brian publicly asked me to pray for him. My heart sank. My hay fever was so bad that this was the last thing I wanted to do. It had been an exhausting enough struggle to teach people the theory, let alone to follow that by actually praying for someone. The devil said, 'Look, you're in no fit state to pray for anyone's healing.' But I did pray for Brian, accidently anointing him with hay fever tears as I did so! He was totally healed within 48 hours. I remained the same.

I had believed in God's power to heal ever since I was a teenager. The question was, 'Should I ask him to heal me?' What if the hay fever was helping to develop my character? Was my affliction doing me some good? Would the Lord prefer me to continue to suffer for some unknown worthwhile goal?

While asking all these questions, I was taking my tablets. If the GP had offered me a tablet that would have produced an instant cure, I would have swallowed it without hesitation. In fact, every Christian who goes to a GP or works in a hospital is saying very loudly to the Lord, 'I believe it's good to be healed and I am working on your side in this battle against illness.' I needed to realise how inconsistent my thinking had been. I was going to a doctor for total healing but when speaking to God I was asking if he really wanted me to remain ill for some unknown mystical reason.

It is important to treat illness as an enemy and never

to make it into a friend. When we are ill the Lord teaches us some important lessons, but we don't *have* to be ill in order to learn those particular lessons. The Lord can teach us the same lessons without our being ill. Unfortunately many people in health adopt a different attitude to God and become unteachable. Similarly, the Lord gives strength to Christians who are tortured for their faith: it would be wrong, however, to claim that there is a particular experience of God's strengthening grace which is limited to people who suffer in that way. So, a healthy person does not lose out at all through being healthy. The grace of God can work just as fully in a healthy person as in a sick person. God never desires that we should be inflicted with illness in order to make it possible for him to do something special in us by his grace.

The life of Jesus Christ illustrates this fully for us. He was described as being 'full of grace'. He experienced continuous good health, while at the same time the grace of God abounded in him in a complete way.

If we do not grasp this truth clearly we will give false positive values to our ill-health. If we have that wrong attitude, we will find ourselves hesitating to ask the Lord to remove from us something which we suspect is working out some good purpose in us. Once my thinking was sorted out, I prayed in an unambiguous way to the Lord, and I was instantly healed.

God's intention
If we realise that God wants us to enjoy full health now – we might wonder whether this has always been God's intention from the beginning of time, and if so, what has gone wrong, and why?

In order to consolidate our faith we need to ask the question: *Has it always been God's intention that all should be whole and healthy?*

The Bible teaches that God created everything and it was perfect. Part of that perfection was man's perfect health. At that time the creation was how God intended it to be. Health and well-being were what God desired for us.

If we look to the future, we are told that God's will for his creation will be fulfilled. What is that will? The scriptures declare that at the end of time creation will be restored to its original perfection and full health to God's people. Our bodies will be perfect. We shall be made whole, and arrive in heaven unblemished (Jude 24).

Today we live between the day of creation and the final day. We live in a world of ill-health. What went wrong? It is a matter of great surprise to many when they are told that what they need if they are to enjoy a healthy life is not just taking medicine but getting their relationships put right. Our relationships affect our well-being. In the beginning, there was a breakdown of the perfect relationship between man and God. Ill-health followed. The breakdown has continued – and so creation is imperfect. On the final day, that relationship will be restored, and the creation made perfect and all the redeemed completely healed.

Let us look at this in more detail and we will see its implications for us in our everyday lives. The relationships we will be examining are between ourselves and God, and within ourselves.

Restored relationships

Why does our well-being depend upon a restoration of our relationship with God? We were originally created to be in fellowship with God. Communication between us and God was intended to be easy and straightforward. We were created to be close to him, and to have no feelings of shame about any part of ourselves or our actions. We were made so that we could enjoy harmonious loving fellowship with God. When that harmony was broken by sin, we desired to hide from God and illness followed. But we are not left hopelessly bemoaning a golden age of perfect health and fellowship with God.

We have something wonderful to which to look forward. At the end of time there will be a new harmony within creation (Is 11.6); tears and suffering will come to an end (Rev 7.17); God will be immediately present with us (Rev 21.1). John saw what would happen:

> Then I saw a new heaven and a new earth, for the first heaven and the first earth had passed away, and there was no longer any sea. . . . I heard a loud voice from the throne saying, 'Now the dwelling of God is with men, and he will live with them. They will be his people, and God himself will be with them and be their God. He will wipe every tear from their eyes. There will be no more death or mourning or crying or pain, for the old order of things has passed away' (Rev 21.1–4).

The day of creation seems a long time ago. And the final day may seem almost as far away into the future. But what about today? We are alive in the time when the old order is in the process of passing away, and the new order is beginning to come. Jesus died to restore the relationship between us and God and his kingly rule over sin and death has already begun. His kingdom has come in power. The fellowship we can have with the Lord now is a wonderful foretaste of fellowship with him in that final new order. The kingdom of God on earth is the life of the world to come invading our existence and re-establishing the relationship between God and man. God is restoring both us and his creation. We have a forestate of heaven even now on earth.

Billy Graham was asked, 'Why don't you pray for the sick in your crusades?' to which he replied that his primary calling was to preach the gospel. He then added that as he does this, frequently people are not only restored to a relationship with God but also healed of their bodily ailments. The new relationship with God brings physical healing.

We are called not just to give intellectual consent to the belief that a new relationship with God has been established for us by Christ's death on the cross; we are called to enjoy *confidence* in this new relationship. By faith and repentance we experience the *assurance* of having been forgiven; we *know* we are reconciled to God by the death of his Son. Like the paralysed man who was lowered through the roof of the house by his believing friends, we have been carried to Jesus and have also heard him say those words of forgiveness which enable us to be made healthy: 'Take heart, your sins are forgiven, get up and walk' (Mt 9.2).

As we experience the reality that God has forgiven us, we are given a confidence in God's desire to bring us to health and wholeness. We become like the psalmist who knew that he was forgiven. The Lord had lifted up

his head, so that he was able to say in effect to him:
'With confidence I can say that you love me; you really
do; I know it'; and sing:

> But you are a shield around me, O Lord,
> my Glorious One, who lifts up my head.
> To the Lord I cry aloud,
> and he answers me from his holy hill (Ps 3.3–4).

No deception
In this confident relationship with God there has
ceased to be a desire to hide anything from him. No
longer do we wish to deceive him. We want to be honest
and open. When there is deception and hiding there can
never be a trusting relationship.

We need to ask, 'Am I hiding from God? Am I open
to him? Am I trying to deceive him?' On the human
level dishonesty ruins relationships. Until there is reconciliation and the resolve not to deceive again people
will find it difficult to look each other straight in the
face. Children often reveal that they have done something wrong by their inability to look a parent in the
eye. It has been said the eye is the window into the soul.
Sometimes if we look someone in the eye that person
may feel that we can see his thoughts. It is hard to look
directly at a person if you are harbouring a grudge
against him. We need to be able to look God in the face.

Satan is the father of lies and deception. Where
he dwells there is a remoteness from God and a loss
of confidence in God's goodness. There develops a
question in the mind: 'Does God desire my healing – or
not?'

When a person cannot look us in the face, this may
indicate that he feels uncomfortable; he may even feel

threatened by us. Similarly, many people feel threatened by God, rather than confident about his love for them; they feel guilty and perceive him only as the God of holy wrath. The unforgiven person rightly feels like this. But if we turn to God and receive his loving forgiveness, we will know that we have been 'saved from the wrath to come'. We will then no longer feel threatened by God's holiness. We will know and enjoy a new relationship with him. We will experience the love that flows with healing power from his very heart. As we allow ourselves to receive it, healing will begin.

Chapter 2

A RECONCILED HEART

What are the effects of being reconciled to God? God's powerful nature will not be changed by any influence we might have on him but it will have profound effects on us. These effects will not be confined to our spiritual aspect; the whole of our being will be changed.

Inner wholeness

This brings us to the question: *How does the restoration of our relationship with God affect our internal wellbeing?*

We have probably all met people who were tense or neurotic until they got married. Thereafter, the love, security and acceptance that their marriage gave them enabled their fears and loneliness to disappear and they became more healed personalities. Healing is even more likely to result from the impact of a restored relationship with the God of love and of the stability of that relationship. After all God's love surpasses human love, and God's dependability is renowned from eternity to eternity. God created us to enjoy a harmonious relationship with him and through that relationship, internal harmony.

The Bible teaches that our humanity is an essential unity of which the body and soul are different aspects; a unity created to reflect harmony. God himself has an 'internal' harmony of Father, Son and Holy Spirit. We are created in the image of God – created therefore to reflect that harmony. The harmony within God is dynamic, and God created us by breathing into us his life-giving breath so that we too could have a dynamic internal harmony: 'Then God said, "Let us make man in our image, in our likeness and let them rule"' (Gen 1.26a). 'The Lord formed man from the dust of the ground and breathed into his nostrils the breath of life, and man became a living being' (Gen 2.7).

We were created to have dignity and moral sensibility, and to delight in the good (Gen 1.31). But after the fall, sin entered humanity and man's nature inclined towards evil. We were created to experience fellowship with God and, in that fellowship, to know inner harmony of body and soul. But that relationship was broken by sin and the image of God was distorted and man experienced spiritual death. The correct way of exercising the rule and authority given to us was also lost. Every part of our being was affected – spiritual, emotional, sexual, mental, social, and physical.

I was amazed, while regularly visiting patients in a hospital to find that in an eye ward one patient was apparently getting no treatment. Other patients were undergoing successful cataract operations which had the effect of instantly transforming their lives. I enquired about this apparently 'neglected' blind patient and was told that her blindness was caused by tension and that she was being given tablets to relax her. Sure enough, a week later when she was totally relaxed, she was able to see again.

We often make the mistake of thinking of ourselves as having separate entities called mind, body and soul. In fact, we are a complex inter-related unity so if one aspect of our being suffers, the others will suffer to some degree also.

The gospel proclaims that the rule of God is being restored and that through this rule we can be healed and saved. On the final day, when Christ's kingdom will be consummated, our healing will be complete. Paul wrote: 'May your whole spirit, soul and body be kept blameless at the coming of our Lord Jesus Christ' (1 Thess 5.23–24).

When Jesus healed someone, he didn't deal with just one aspect of the condition. He wanted to bring healing to the totality of that person. He knew that physical bodies would only stay healthy where there was spiritual health too.

Jesus taught about the nature of man and God by demonstrating the truth of what he said. Jesus was a whole man united with the fulness of God. From birth onwards, Jesus was whole at all levels – mentally, physically, spiritually and socially; he was totally living a harmonious life with himself, with God and with his fellow man. We read of his childhood: 'And the child grew and became strong; he was filled with wisdom, and the grace of God was upon him'; and again: 'And Jesus grew in wisdom [*mentally*] and stature [*physically*] and in favour with God [*spiritually*] and man [*socially*]' (Lk 1.40, 52). Jesus all through his life demonstrated total wholeness.

After a church service in York a young woman whom

we did not know at all, came to my wife and me and asked for prayer for her painful back. It had been in that condition for six years, she told us. We first prayed in silence asking the Lord for some insight into the problem. Then the Lord told me to pray aloud for a healing of the woman's relationship with her father. I did so – and she just melted into tears. We carried on praying along these lines for a while. Afterwards as she was walking away, I called after her, 'How is your back?' She seemed to have forgotten about it. But then she called back, 'Yes, it's perfect, no pain at all.'

God desires to heal us – but he starts with that aspect of our total being which he sees to be the best starting point and not necessarily where *we* would start.

We may be convinced from scripture of God's original and final plan to have a perfect world in which man has confident relationship with God and perfect harmony within his own being. But we may still be unconvinced that God heals people today.

Does God heal today?

Some people believe the Bible when it says that Jesus performed miracles of healing. They may even believe that when the early disciples prayed for the sick, they were miraculously healed. They might add, however, that after the apostolic age miracles were no longer necessary because the authority of the apostles and their writing were finally acknowledged.

But there seems to be no special reverence for the authority of the apostles today. The need to convince people of the authority of Christ and of the scripture seems just as great today as it ever was. In any case, to argue that miracles were needed to authenticate Jesus and the apostles is to miss the main point of Jesus' healing ministry. The healings were first, and foremost, an expression of Jesus' overflowing love and compassion for people. He desired to help them in a practical way. That desire of Jesus remains unchanging.

Many still need his healing touch today, and it is still the desire of his heart to heal people. We, personally, might find it difficult to believe in miracles of healing today, but this does not give us the right to impose a limit on the relevance of some verses of scripture to our modern times.

The modern difficulty in believing in Jesus' healing power is just a new expression of an old difficulty. Throughout the centuries it has been met, and is still being met, with sensitivity by Jesus.

We should reflect his attitude when we meet people who are unsure as to whether or not God wants to heal them. We read of Jesus going to the pool of Bethesda (Jn 5.1ff). One invalid had been there for thirty-eight years. Jesus asked, 'Do you want to be healed?' The man replied that his situation was hopeless – he had no-one to help him. He was unaware of the fact that he was saying these things to the very person for whom no situation is hopeless and who can always help. Jesus' response was to say to the man, 'Get up! Pick up your mat and walk.' At once he was cured: '. . . he picked up his mat and walked.'

When Jesus asks you, 'Do you want to be healed?' just simply say 'Yes, Lord,' because he is willing to heal you, and he has the power to do so, today.

God's way of healing

We may be reconciled to God, but we may still be

unreconciled to the way God desires to bring healing to us. Often it is our unwillingness to be healed God's way which is the problem. Our pride may hold us back because we don't want to receive healing from God by faith alone. It may be that when God has blessed a church by healing people, the Christians start wanting to *contribute* to the process of healing – by working up the right atmosphere, for instance. This means that fewer and fewer people are healed, because man in his pride has started believing that God needs help to do the supernatural. Similarly, individuals who have begun to be healed by God sometimes revert to their previous condition, or block God's healing work, by actions and attitudes indicating that they think God needs their help.

It is interesting that many people whom the Lord uses most consistently in the healing ministry, are aware of a time in their ministry when they prayed for the sick but without achieving results or even with the effect of making people worse. They had to get to a point where it became obvious to them that they of themselves had absolutely nothing to offer. Often a painful time would follow when the Lord had to deal with their pride; but the Lord was teaching them the lesson that divine healing is all of *grace* and not of merit or human ability.

If you have witnessed an occasion when God healed someone miraculously, you will realise that all you did was to express your faith in the fact that God delights to heal. You became aware of God's desire to express his love through healing. You expressed that in prayer and someone was healed.

I once remember a student coming to me at the end

of a long service. I was very tired and feeling not at all spiritual. She insisted that I should pray with her and, remembering a verse from James which says that the elders '*will* pray for the sick', I reluctantly did so. She had a painful back condition. I prayed, just because, however unspiritual I felt, I couldn't get away from God's promises in scripture. She was immediately healed and I was totally amazed. Those ten seconds taught me a great deal.

'The prayer of faith will heal the sick' (Jas 5.14, 15). Praying for the sick is very uncomplicated. It needs no expertise. When God gives you the gift of faith that he is going to heal someone, you pray for them and the Lord heals them. It's as simple as that. It really is. In ministry I often reflect on how difficult it is for me to be simple.

Side-tracked by methods

We must avoid being side-tracked into believing that it is this or that method which works, whether it be the automatic recitation of various prayers and words from scripture or the psychological approach. A clear trusting prayer directed to the Lord is all that is necessary, as we open to the spontaneous working of the Holy Spirit and keep ourselves in the background. Where this does not happen, there emerges a 'professional' group of healers who come to be regarded as experts in a particular way of healing.

God wants his reconciled people to express faith in him. He gives us faith and expects us to trust that he desires to heal. 'According to your faith will it be done to you' (Mt 9.29). The healing comes as we express faith in the Lord and his desire to heal. He has promised to grant 'whatever you ask in *my name*'.

Asking in the name of Jesus is not to use the name 'Jesus' as if it were some lucky charm having power in itself; rather we are saying that we are praying for healing out of a positive relationship to Jesus' character. His name represents his character. So we pray out of a relationship in which we are not trying to manipulate God into conforming with our way of thinking but expressing confidence in his love and grace and asking him to express his love in one particular way. We are not persuading but rather resting in him. Jesus said: 'Whatever you ask for in prayer, believe that you have received it, and it will be yours' (Mk 11.24).

After *praying* how do we continue to express that confidence in God's love? 'Devote yourselves to prayer, being watchful and thankful' (Col 4.2). This is a call to express faith in God *before* there is the evidence of healing; faith that God was sincere when he made the promises recorded in the Bible; faith that waits for the fulfilment of those promises.

As well as continuing in prayer, we are to give thanks to God for his commitment to heal us and, as we wait, keep our eyes open. We are to watch prayerfully and see what happens. Often there is immediate evidence of some degree of improvement, however small, in the spiritual, mental, emotional or physical aspect of our being. We then concentrate on that rather than on the other areas.

Often, where physical ailments are stress-related, the Lord heals the person's state of mind first. For example we may pray for someone to be healed of arthritis. There may be no physical transformation immediately but we may find that a new peace has descended on that person; the peace of God has filled them. At this point we have evidence of the desire of the Lord to heal the person, so we continue in prayer – watching what is happening and giving thanks for God's loving nature at work to change the person's condition.

Be reconciled to the fact that God desires to heal us. Let us not have doubts about this. If we are ill, God wants to heal us. Look at his promises which are fully backed up by God's own character. To deny that God is as good as his word is to call him a liar, and we would not want to do that. John wrote: 'But you have an anointing from the Holy One, and all of you know the truth. I do not write to you because you do not know the truth, but because you do know it and because no lie comes from the truth' (1 Jn 2.20, 21).

Watch and pray

If the Lord has given us faith that these promises apply to us personally then let us act upon it. In prayer let us express confidence in God's desire to heal us individually. We need very specifically to ask the Lord to manifest his love by healing whatever needs to be healed. We should ask him to be actively with us and in us for our healing. Then we must watch what happens both in our spirit and in our body; all the while praising the Lord, continuing in prayer, watching and giving thanks.

Let's not pretend that we have received more healing than we have. There is no need to exaggerate: it does not help us or bring glory to God; instead, it could suggest that God is working too slowly. If we believe that God answers our prayer, we can wait for the full application of his answer. The man mentioned in the introduction, who had a replacement hip, had to learn to enter into the reality of what the surgeon had done for him, but he was never encouraged to believe that he was not in pain when he was still in agony.

On one occasion I prayed for someone who had a terrible headache. As we walked away from the prayer meeting, I asked him how he was. He replied, 'My headache has gone, but all the symptoms are still there.' My profound theological reply was 'That's rubbish!' I did not want him to live in a world of make-believe. There was nothing constructive in his pretending to be better than he was. He still had a bad headache. His healing had not yet come. My comment actually made him feel much better, because he was able to acknowledge the reality of the situation and then wait patiently for the easing of the pain, believing that God was at work in him to bring this about soon.

Pray and *watch*. God *will* have done something in answer to your prayer. How can we be sure? Just because he promised. He wants to heal you.

The creation is fallen because of sin, and so we experience bad health. In heaven there will be no sickness or pain. But in the present, at this very moment, as God's reconciled people, we can enter into a foretaste of heaven, because the kingdom of heaven is here among us and healing is a sign of its presence. Jesus said, 'Heal the sick who are there and tell them, "The kingdom of God is near you"' (Lk 10.9).

Chapter 3

THE HEART OF THE MATTER –
THE CROSS

Life through an execution

Has it ever struck you as strange that the Christian
faith, with its stress on the importance of love, should
have as its hallmark a symbol of brutal torture
and death? The cross is the sign above nearly every
Christian place of worship. Inside many churches it
provides the central visible focal point. It is worn on
lapels or hung on chains round people's necks.

Can't we think of something better than the symbol
of death to represent our faith? No. Without the cross
we know that we are totally lost; our only hope is
through the cross.

Sometimes the cross has a representation of Christ on
it; this reminds us of the horror of the death which Jesus
died for us. The cross is the sign of shame; it is the place
where outrageous criminals were executed as a result of
society's judgement on them as being unfit to live in a
civilised community.

Sometimes the cross has no figure on it, reminding us
that Jesus has risen from the dead and is alive and with
us now. The cross is the place of the victory of God's

love over our human hatred of him: God's victory over our sin and our consequent lack of wholeness. The cross is central in a healthy attitude to God, because it constantly reminds us that it was necessary for Christ to die for us; and we need to be reminded that God loves us so much that he was prepared to go to such great lengths for us.

Human pride rejects the cross as the way to health. Such pride is an unhealthy aspect of our human nature. It can be at the heart of some of our anxieties and irrational fears. It can rob us of a peace which is a prerequisite of a sense of wellbeing. It can cause us to think that all this talk about the cross of Christ and of his blood shed for us, is rather distasteful. We would prefer to think that we weren't bad enough to justify God having to go to such great lengths to save us. But the Bible says that unless we repent of our sin and come humbly to the cross for forgiveness, then we will lack wholeness eternally.

We might like to think that all we need to do is to try harder to live like Christ – but God declares that we are so fallen that there is no hope of us succeeding in that quest, and that the first thing we need to recognise is our need to be redeemed. The cross of Christ shouts out that such sinners need God's redeeming love which alone can rescue us and make and keep us whole.

The cross speaks of our helplessness, of our need to die to all our attempts at redeeming ourselves and to choose to be open to God's power; it speaks of our rebellion against God and of our need to let our rebellious nature be crucified, and to come humbly in faith to receive God's forgiveness. Christ was crucified for us and so provided the means by which we can be crucified with him and see our old nature being put to death by God. In the words of Isaac Watts' hymn:

> When I survey the wondrous cross
> On which the Prince of Glory died,
> My richest gain I count but loss
> And pour contempt on all my pride.

Perfect sacrifice

Our representatives crucified Jesus Christ because his perfection was a threat to them. Pilate, Herod and the crowds felt threatened because Jesus' life and words revealed their wrong attitude to God, one another and life in general. They wanted to get rid of the One who revealed, by his own very different life and attitude, their own shallowness, hypocrisy, compromise and sickness of being. The life of Jesus offered on the cross was a life of perfection and wholeness; nothing was left undone which should have been done. Jesus could cry 'It is finished,' or 'It is completed.'

But there is another sense in which this shout was a cry of victory. Jesus was also saying that our way back to God had been completed. Jesus had removed every obstacle in our pathway. The power of sin over our lives and Satan's hold on us had been broken. The full price of our redemption had been paid so that we could walk in newness of life, with a new freedom and wholeness.

The words 'It is finished' used to be stamped on a bill showing that it had been paid in full, so that the holder would not be requested to pay again. The same words also used to be stamped on a prisoner's hand when he had paid his full sentence and was being released, so that if he was subsequently stopped in the street he could show clear evidence of his right to be free.

Similarly, the price for our redemption has been paid; we now have a right to be free. Enjoy this new reality! The truth and relevance of Christ's death was seen to be so central by the early church that parts of Isaiah 53.3–6 are quoted more than fifty times in the New Testament!

> He was despised and rejected by men:
> a man of sorrows, and acquainted with grief;
> and as one from whom men hide their faces
> he was despised, and we esteemed him not.
> Surely he has born our griefs and carried our sorrows;
> yet we esteemed him stricken, smitten by God, and
>   afflicted.
> But he was wounded for our transgressions;
> he was bruised for our iniquities;
> upon him was the chastisement that made us whole, and
>   with his stripes we are healed.
> All we like sheep have gone astray;
> we have turned every one to his own way;
> and the Lord has laid on him the iniquity of us all.

We must realise three benefits from Christ's death: that we are redeemed, purified and justified by the blood of Christ.

Redemption

We are redeemed by the blood of Christ. 'It was not with perishable things such as silver or gold that you were redeemed . . . but with the precious blood of Christ' (1 Pet 1.18, 19). The Bible informs us that the reality is that Jesus died to 'redeem' or buy us back. Frequently we hear of kidnappings where a ransom is demanded for the redemption of someone. The same applies to us. *We* were kidnapped and no longer free to return home to God. A price had to be paid for our ransom. That price was not as cheap as silver or gold; it was too high a price for us to pay so Christ paid it by his death. No wonder Charles Wesley wrote:

Amazing love, how can it be,
That thou my God shouldst die for me

We need to have a deep sense of gratitude for what God has done for us. A mother out of love for her little daughter saved her from a house on fire but, in doing so, her hands got badly burnt. When the girl grew up, she had no idea why her mother's hands were so disfigured and was ashamed of the way they looked. So she always asked her to keep her hands covered with gloves. One day the daughter asked her mother to tell her how her hands got into that condition. Her mother told her. The child wept tears of gratitude, and then said, 'Oh mother, these are beautiful hands, the most beautiful in the world. Don't ever hide them again.' The daughter had a deep gratitude for something that previously seemed very ugly.

Do you find the cross beautiful? Stop a moment to pray and simply ask Jesus Christ *why* he was nailed to the cross. The New Testament emphasis on the redeeming blood of Jesus may at first seem to be almost repulsive. We need to think again, just as the little girl needed to learn the true beauty of her mother's hands. We need to become deeply grateful to Jesus for dying for us. This gratitude will increase as we come to realise that, through his death, our old lives have been put to death as well. We have been crucified with Christ. If we know that we have actually died with Christ and been

raised again with him, then the words of the old Holy
Communion service will fill us with awesome wonder.
'Draw near and receive the body of our Lord Jesus
Christ, which was given for you; and his blood which
was shed for you. Take this in remembrance that Christ
died for you, and feed on him in your hearts by faith
with thanksgiving.' We are redeemed from our old
futile ways by the blood of Christ.

Purification

We are purified by the blood of Christ. To have healing
and life in all its fullness we need also to realise that the
blood of Christ purifies us. 'The blood of Christ . . . will
purify your conscience from dead works to serve the
living God' (Heb 9.14). The blood of Christ purifies the
conscience. Nobody has a totally clear conscience by
nature. The conscience sits in judgement over every
thought, word and deed. It can be very sensitive or,
through constant repression, very insensitive. We will
be only too aware that we cannot look back over our
life without some sense of guilt over what we have
thought, said, or done. Memories of these things
can haunt us and make us ill-at-ease. They certainly
don't help us to look forward to the final Judgement
Day.

Our conscience will not be silenced *but* the Bible
teaches that it can be *purified*. Through the cross it *is*
possible to know that our past is in the past, put to
death with Christ and buried with him. We need to
realise that we *are* cut off from the past; that we have a
new start as a *new* person. If we were to liken our past
lives to a car, then we could say that God doesn't give
the car a re-conditioned engine; he creates a new

vehicle. God does not just give us a new start; he also gives us a new life to start with. In other words, God does not re-condition our hearts and consciences; rather, he makes us into new people.

Justification

We are justified by the blood of Christ. Redeemed and purified by the death of Christ, we are also justified by his blood (Rom 5.9). To be justified means that we are set free from blame and from the consequences of our previous actions in God's sight. When Jesus was crucified, he was probably crucified on the cross prepared for Barabbas, a notorious criminal. The crowd, asked by Pilate to choose between Barabbas and Jesus, wanted Barabbas' life to be spared and Jesus to be crucified. So Jesus died on Barabbas' cross; he died in the place of Barabbas. If Barabbas had been there at the scene of the crucifixion of Jesus, he would have been saying to himself, 'I should have been there; that's what I deserved; Jesus is dying there in my place.'

We can look at the cross of Christ and say those same words with equal truth: 'I should have been there; that's what I deserve; Jesus has died in my place.' Jesus took the consequences of our sin and, since sin separates us from God, Jesus felt separated from his Father when he cried out, 'My God, my God, why have you forsaken me?' (Mt 27.46; Mk 15.34).

In a far deeper sense than Barabbas could have realised, we owe our well-being, our health and our freedom to find God, to the death of Jesus. We have been justified by his blood, and our guilt and blame have been dealt with once and for all; through faith in Jesus' death for us we can know that God accepts us as though we had never sinned. Jesus bore the judgement so that we can be set free to enjoy our new life of fellowship with God.

An American Indian tribe that camped in the wide open prairies had a saying: 'The fire cannot come where the fire has already been.' Whenever great fires came sweeping across the prairies devouring everything in their path and moving relentlessly towards them, they would light a fire and burn the prairie around their camp so that the advancing fire, having nothing to feed on, would be stopped before reaching and utterly consuming them.

The fire of judgement against sin, the fire of being eternally separated from God, cannot consume us, because there on the cross the fire has already burnt. It burnt to save us. Jesus died in our place. We have nothing to fear. We who are redeemed and purified and justified by our Lord Jesus Christ are saved *from* the fire, and saved *into* health and well-being in an eternal fellowship with God the Father.

To *enjoy* real wholeness in Christ we must begin by realising what Christ has achieved for us. The cross of Christ brings wholeness of life to those who humble themselves, accept the guilt of being responsible for having Jesus crucified, see their old life as having ended there, and then start living in the reality of their new life as the redeemed, purified and justified people of God.

It is only then that we are going to find real mental, emotional, physical and spiritual health and wholeness. We all need to dwell on this achievement until it affects us at real depth. We need to realise that certain things are no longer relevant to a true understanding of our ongoing situation. But the devil, who is called the father of lies, wants to keep us from this true understanding, as we shall see in the next chapter.

Chapter 4

A GUILT-RIDDEN HEART

Do we carry about with us feelings of guilt which we should have discarded long since? Do we therefore accuse ourselves of being very sub-standard and get annoyed with ourselves because of the frequency with which unworthy thoughts pass through our mind?

'Am I really a Christian?' you may ask yourself. 'Am I really a "new creation"?' There seem to be so many of the old thought-patterns still remaining.

As far as we know we have brought before the Lord everything we have done wrong. We recognise our sinfulness, and have repented of what we have done and been. We know that when we confessed these things, God was faithful and cleansed and forgave us and gave us a new life to live. Nevertheless, we cannot help asking ourselves, 'Am I really any different? Have I really changed?'

These nagging questions undermine our confidence in the possibility of ever improving. We start to doubt whether we will ever become the sort of people God wants us to be, or live at the spiritual level to which we are called, or minister in the Lord and in his power.

Negative thoughts come at us like bullets shot from an automatic rifle. The rapid hail is alarming and comes with destructive force, attacking the very heart of our personality and bringing inner disharmony which in turn, brings disharmony in our relationships with others. Why do we think like this?

The devil's nature and tactics

We need to realise that we have a full-time accuser: the devil (Rev 12.10). He puts all manner of evil suggestions into our minds. But don't let that alarm us. The fact that these things are happening does not mean that we are demonised. Rather we are experiencing what happens to all Christians who are seriously wanting to follow their Lord.

Notice what happened to Jesus Christ himself. All sorts of evil thoughts passed into his mind. Yes – the pure and Holy Son of God was tempted in every way as we are. He was even tempted to get involved in devil-worship. Does this shock us? If it does, it is only because we are not used to recognising the voice of the devil when he speaks to us. The temptations came to Jesus not at a time when he was at a low ebb but immediately after he had been empowered by the Holy Spirit for his future ministry.

Jesus remained pure and holy. He did not sin. Nor did he accuse *himself* for having such thoughts. Instead, immediately recognising the voice of the devil, he rebuked him. 'Get behind me Satan.' Then he applied the objective truth of God's word in counter-attack. We, like Jesus himself, need to recognise that the *truth* is always on our side. The more we apply it the healthier we will become.

Do *we* recognise the devil's activity? It is essential to do so if we are to defeat satanic influence in our life, and if we are not to be robbed of our effectiveness for God. Before an important fight, the boxers look at video tapes of their opponents in action. They study their style, their habits, their strengths and weaknesses. Let's remember that *we* are in a fight against the devil. It is not a fight we had to go looking for: the devil has long ago declared himself our dedicated enemy. He took the initiative and is on a continuous drive to overthrow us. We are in a warfare situation, so we need to recognise the devil's tactics and be alert. The apostle Paul tells us to put on the whole armour of God. Then we will be defended from all the attacks of the enemy, and having fought against him, will still be standing at the end of the battle. Most of the armour is for defence. Even the sword of the Spirit, which is the word of God, counter-attacks by overcoming falsehood with truth.

One way that the word of God does this is by revealing the devil's nature and by removing his cover. The devil tries to fight us under various disguises and camouflages. He will even pretend to be an angel of light (2 Cor 11.14). The scriptures also enlighten us about the devil's strategy and aims. Even if he doesn't succeed in getting us to act upon the temptation, he will not give up. He will return to accuse us of being guilty for even thinking those thoughts in the first place – the very thoughts that he himself suggested to our minds! If we do not realise that this is what the devil does we will probably walk under the burden of feelings of false guilt which we should never have.

What then is the devil like? What are his ambitions? What does he hope to achieve in this battle against us?

It is impossible to give a comprehensive description of
the devil because our minds are too limited to register
the complete reality of his depravity. His desire is to
undermine us by endless accusations. He continually
and relentlessly desires to tear us apart. He is not gentle
in this. He is ruthless in trying to make us feel un-
necessarily guilty. He is like a savage, powerful, wild
animal which pounces on its prey, tearing it apart so as
to devour it. To realise these things and do nothing
would be plain stupidity. The apostle Peter calls us to
recognise the devil for who he is – our powerful adver-
sary. 'Be self-controlled and alert. Your enemy the devil
prowls around like a roaring lion, looking for someone
to devour. Resist him' (1 Pet 5.8–9).

God treats us so very differently. Yes, he may reveal
things to us about ourselves, things which may make us
feel guilty. But *at the same time* he always gives us the
power to repent and be transformed. God does not want
us to grovel before him in utter despair. He is like the
forgiving father in the parable of the Prodigal Son. The
son, returning home, prepared to say that he had
sinned and was unworthy and would be happy to be
taken on as a hired servant, is cut short by his father
who has *run* to meet and embrace him. God is like that.
The Holy Spirit only reveals something to us *at the very
moment* that God is there to transform the situation
wonderfully.

The devil's activity is in absolute contrast to this. He
accuses us, often with lies, trying to make us feel a
despairing and hopeless guilt and so give up being a
disciple of Jesus Christ. The devil comes to tear our
character apart. If we do not co-operate with him, he
will try to discredit us in the eyes of other people, so that

they can add their accusing voice to his own. The very word 'devil' comes from the word 'slanderer'.

Firstly – he will slander us to ourselves, giving us a distorted picture of ourselves. If we are Christians the most significant thing about us is the glorious fact that we are *children of God*. We should want to jump with joy as we realise that fact. My own son at the age of four used to jump for joy when he unexpectedly met me in the street while returning home with his mother. I am sure I didn't deserve such enthusiasm, but I loved seeing it! We are children of God. Just think about it. Doesn't it make us want to jump for joy? God loves to see us react like that to him, and deserves such a reaction from us.

But the devil hates to see this. He will come and try to make us feel so full of guilt that a heaviness comes upon our souls and we begin to think that the most significant things about ourselves are the problems we have. This is a lie and we need to recognise its origin. He wants to distort the image we have of ourselves, making it seem completely incompatible with being a genuine Christian. He wants to undermine our belief in God's promises and crowd our minds with hundreds of reasons why we will always be a failure and remain sub-standard.

Secondly, the devil will distort other people's view of us. When we have done something with pure and holy motives and people have attributed to us base motives, haven't we sighed to ourselves and said, 'How could they have believed such evil of me?' The answer, of course, is that the devil has been active.

Our opponent is no weakling that can easily be dismissed. The apostle Paul says: 'It is not against human enemies that we have to struggle, but against the sovereignties and powers who originate the darkness in this world, the spiritual army of evil in the heavens' (Eph 6.12, *Jerusalem Bible*).

The devil will use anybody to be his mouthpiece, but we struggle or wrestle not against them – but against *him*. Wrestling is a very strenuous activity. Wrestlers engage one another in close physical combat. There is much expenditure of energy. There is a meeting of opposing strong muscles. There is grunting and perspiration. There is the attempt to make limbs of the body bend in ways they were not created to bend. When we wrestle with the devil we cannot do so in a detached way. There is close personal involvement; the powers against which we wrestle are always trying to bring darkness into the intellectual, spiritual and moral realms.

The devil is subtle: he is no blundering idiot. He is the expert at disguise and so deceives many people into believing that he is even an angel of light. In this guise, he gets them off-guard and tries to win them over to his service and also bring about their own final destruction. To this end, he is as subtle as a serpent and quietly works among people to make them blind to the truth and to keep them away from the path that God wants them to walk in. The apostle John writes: 'The whole world is in the power of the evil one' (1 Jn 5.19).

Do we need to make some mental adjustment to our way of thinking in order to take that statement seriously? The Evil One came into God's glorious world which was created perfect, bringing such pain and suffering and such moral and spiritual deformity, that it is no longer recognised as *God's* world by millions of people today. The devil is more evil than we can imagine: proud, cruel, scornful, hateful, vile and despicable. He undermines, discredits and perverts. He is energetically recruiting more and more followers, some of whom even proudly announce that they worship him. Let us heed the warning of the book of Revelation: 'The devil has come down to you in great wrath, because he knows his time is short' (Rev 12.12). In the time available he wants to destroy our lives and paralyse us spiritually by piling upon us guilt feelings. To this end he will be found accusing us day and night – continually (Rev 12.10).

Defeated enemy

The last word, however, is not with the devil but with Jesus Christ. If we need to know our enemy so as to recognise his voice (which we do), how much more do we need to recognise our Friend – the Lord Jesus Christ. Left in the hands of the enemy, the future would be very gloomy and full of bad news. We would be far away from wholeness because we would be twisted up with fear and feelings of guilt. We need a gospel. We need to hear and absorb the good news that Jesus, the fighter, has defeated the devil. There is hope for the future. There can be a future full of joy and a life lived in the absence of guilt feelings. The victory of Christ on the cross shows that God is ultimately in control. The devil might be on a long chain – but he *is* chained and bound. We need to walk by this reality as did Christian in *Pilgrim's Progress*:

> And looking very narrowly before him as he went, he espied two lions in the way. Now, thought he, I see the danger that Mistrust and Timorous were driven back by. (The lions were chained, but he saw not the chains.) Then

he was afraid, and thought nothing but death was before him; but the porter at the lodge, whose name is Watchful, perceiving that Christian made a halt as if he would go back, cried unto him, saying, 'Is thy strength so small? (Mk 4.40). Fear not the lions, for they are chained, and are placed there for trial of faith where it is; and for the discovery of those that have none: keep in the midst of the path, and no hurt shall come unto thee.' Then I saw that he went on, trembling for fear of the lions, but taking good heed to the directions of the porter. He heard them roar, but they did him no harm.

For our wellbeing and peace of mind, we too need to realise that the powers against us are chained. John Calvin said that however active the devil and the demons were, everywhere they go they have to drag their chains with them. The apostle John triumphantly declares of Jesus: 'The reason the Son of God appeared was to destroy the works of the devil' (1 Jn 3.8b). Our lives should be proclaiming joyfully that he succeeded.

Victorious saviour

Jesus himself was tempted throughout his ministry by the devil. The same word used of his being *tempted* in the wilderness is used of the religious leaders coming with trick questions to tempt him. These religious leaders were being used by the devil himself in an attempt to discredit the ministry and authority of Jesus, but with singular lack of success. The devil tried time and again; he tried to wear Jesus out, but Jesus was victorious every time.

We must not be worn out by temptation. In a strange way we can even be encouraged by the fact that the devil tempts us, and uses other people to be agents of his temptations. The devil 'lets sleeping dogs lie'; he does not disturb them because they are doing no good. When someone becomes a disciple of Jesus Christ then he concentrates his attack on them, as he concentrated his attack on their Master. The Lord himself can use the fact that we are tempted to mature our Christian character. James wrote: 'Count it pure joy, my brothers, whenever you face trials of many kinds, because you know that the testing of your faith develops perseverance. Perseverance must finish its work so that you may be mature and complete, not lacking anything' (Jas 1.2–4).

Jesus persevered and declared the downfall of the kingdom of darkness as he himself brought in the kingdom of God. Demons had to loose their hold on people at the authoritative command of Jesus, and people were set free to enter into wholeness of life and health. Jesus was victorious at every turning of his life, and finally triumphed in his death on the cross. There God 'disarmed the principalities and powers and made a public example of them, triumphing over them in him' (Col 2.5). This was so decisive a victory that the devil was finally dethroned, and the victory of Jesus Christ was openly declared by his resurrection from the dead. This victory was wonderfully and dramatically applied to individuals, and today can be applied to us, individually, as we pray for the outpouring of the Holy Spirit upon ourselves.

This same Holy Spirit is as much with us now as on the day of Pentecost. He is ready today to apply the victory of Jesus over the devil to our lives, so that we can experience a new freedom from the power of the devil's oppressing and depressing activity and from the sting of his constant accusations. Through receiving the power of the Holy Spirit in our lives we can really believe that the *most significant* thing about ourselves is that we are set free and that we have entered the glorious liberty of the children of God. This was the gospel Paul preached, and which we can receive for ourselves. Live in the reality of Paul's words: 'Jesus has delivered us from the dominion of darkness and transferred us to the kingdom of his beloved Son' (Col 1.13).

In summary then, it becomes clear that to enjoy wholeness in Christ, we need to recognise the voice of our enemy – the accuser; to be aware of the nature of the devil; to realise that he is our defeated enemy, to rejoice that we have a victorious Saviour who has brought us out of darkness into his marvellous light. The victory of Christ can be experienced afresh in our lives as we come to him to be cleansed and restored. Jesus will take us, heal us and immerse us in the power of the Holy Spirit. The power of God will enable us to live victoriously – sharing the victory of Christ himself, and living in the forgiveness, light and love of God's presence with us.

> And you, who were dead in trespasses . . . God made alive together with Christ, having forgiven us all our trespasses, having cancelled the bond which stood against us with its legal demands; this he set aside, nailing it to the cross. He disarmed the principalities and powers and made a public example of them, triumphing over them in the cross (Col 2.13–15).

In other words – our God reigns!

Chapter 5

AN IMPRISONED HEART

To be free from bondage, most of us need not only to be delivered from the power of the enemy as described in the previous chapter, but also set free from a *mould* into which other people and circumstances have forced us.

Some of these moulds are easily recognised as detrimental to our wellbeing: others are more subtle. For example, we might admire certain heroes of the faith. We might even wish to be like them and say to ourselves, 'If only we had their giftedness or their spiritual authority, then so much more could be achieved for the Lord in our particular circumstances.' We might then start thinking of our own lives as of little value. Those who do long to be someone else need to see the harmful effects it has on their lives and to ask for the power of the Lord to enable them to change their attitudes.

That the Lord can change us completely in this respect is illustrated wonderfully by the way Jacob, the Old Testament patriarch was so utterly transformed.

Jacob the cheat

Jacob was someone who wanted to be someone else. His father was Isaac – a man who seemed to lack originality. After all, he just dug up the same old wells as his father, Abraham, had and he made the same mistakes in Egypt, too. Perhaps these were things about his father that Jacob could not admire. His mother, Rebekah, on the other hand, seemed to be very different: determined to be a winner in life. Months before Jacob was even born, she was told by God that she would have twins: each child would be the father of a nation but the elder would serve the younger. Rebekah was determined to be on the winning side so Jacob became her favourite son.

The day for the delivery of the twins arrived. Esau was born first, looking very red, then Jacob, holding Esau's heel. So Jacob was given his name which means supplanter, cheat, grabber. Imagine having a name like that! Imagine what it would do to you from early childhood onwards. No doubt Jacob's name became a family joke. If so, he would have had to endure, in acute embarrassment, the telling and re-telling of the story of how the name originated. Each telling of this story would have conditioned him to think of himself as the supreme cheat. The mould of this unpleasant identity would have been set for him.

To make things worse, his father, Isaac, clearly loved Esau, his brother, far more than he loved him. Isaac saw Esau as a man's man: someone who was strong and fit. His wife, Rebekah, however, loved Jacob more than Esau. Jacob was gentle and pale and had soft skin. So, added to the lasting effect of being called 'the cheat' from birth, was the harmful effect of parental favouritism within a family.

Given those circumstances, it was not surprising that Jacob lived up to his name, as two stories from his life illustrate well. The first was when Esau came back hungry from hunting in the countryside. Jacob offered him some food in exchange for the promise of his birthright. In this way, true to the way he had been moulded, he cheated his brother. The second time that Jacob lived up to people's bad expectations of him was when, with his mother's help, he cheated Esau out of his father's blessing. On this occasion, he tried to take on someone else's identity by disguising himself. When his half-blind father said, 'Who are you my son?' Jacob answered, 'I am Esau.' And Isaac blessed him with the blessing meant for Esau.

The question, 'Who are you?' could produce a name for an answer, but the question of our real identity is not so easily given. It might require much heart searching. Like Jacob, we may not be sure who we really are. We want to be *ourselves* but all the forces of our background may forbid us that freedom; we may feel that we have to live up to other people's expectations or we may feel that we must react against them. But, either way, we are not really enjoying the freedom to be ourselves and we cannot break free from our bondage without help.

Another problem Jacob had was that he couldn't relate to other people. His background made it hard to have easy relationships with people. His brother Esau hated him and had every reason for that attitude. But Jacob didn't only have problems with him: he had become a person who found it difficult to relate in a healthy way to *anyone*. People who are striving so hard to be someone they aren't not only put a strain on themselves but also distance themselves from others. There is the strain of continually acting a part, and that of being isolated from other people. Those who try to get to know such people find that they can't get past the mask to meet the *real* person underneath.

Jacob's difficulty in relationships is seen with his brother, his father, and, later, in his strained relationship within his marriage. He proved the truth of the saying that what you sow you reap; if you cheat others, they will try to cheat you. Jacob the cheater was out-cheated by Laban when he tricked him into marrying his older daughter rather than the younger one whom Jacob loved. Jacob treated his wife badly. Then he married Laban's other daughter, Rachel, whom he really loved, but it's interesting that Laban gave Jacob a stern warning about not ill-treating his wives. 'If you ill-treat my daughters . . . remember that God is a witness between you and me' (Gen 31.50).

The story of Jacob is of someone bound by a history of bad relationships: with his brother, father, wives and finally with his father-in-law whom he spent twenty years trying to out-cheat.

Decisive encounter

Then something happened which resulted in a changed identity for him. Years earlier, Jacob had been asked by his dying father, 'Who are you?' and he had cheated and said 'I am Esau.' But when God asked him the same question Jacob was aware that he could not hide his true identity from the Lord and answered, 'Jacob – the cheat.' This indicated that he had started being honest about himself. God often waits until this happens before pouring his healing grace upon us.

Jacob had to face reality. He had reached a point of personal crisis and powerlessness. He couldn't afford to pretend any longer. He felt that his past was catching him up and was about to overwhelm him. His brother, Esau was coming to meet him. This time Esau was not alone; he was marching with four hundred men. Jacob was scared. He sent gifts to Esau in order to soften him up. But Jacob still panicked. What if they were not enough? He sent more gifts as a bribe, to pay him off. But would his brother be bought off? Jacob was absolutely scared for his life.

Then something happened to Jacob that he could never have anticipated. 'A man wrestled with him' (Gen 32.24). His whole life seemed under threat; his thigh was dislocated and he had to hobble about. But he became aware of entering into a new reality; he realised that, in some mysterious way, God himself was involved in the struggle against him; and God struggles with each one of us, to bring us into the world of reality about ourselves and our attitudes to others.

Although Jacob was exhausted, he just clung on, and cried, 'I will not let you go unless you bless me.' Often the Lord waits to hear this persistent cry from us. Jacob still wanted a *blessing*. He was the same man: still desperate to be blessed, still as ambitious as ever, but he showed those qualities in a different way. Now he wanted an *honest* blessing. No longer was he a cheat pretending to be someone else in order to ask for a blessing. So when he was asked for his identity – 'What is your name?' – he replied, 'Jacob' (the cheat); the person who cheated others out of their blessings; the one who was so keen to be in someone else's shoes that he had been acting a part for years.

Then he heard the voice say, 'Your name shall no longer be called Jacob but Israel, for you have striven with God and have prevailed.' Through that encounter with the Lord, Israel, alias Jacob, was made a real man. He had seen the face of the Lord: his true life had been preserved and the falsehood consumed. He had admitted, to the living Lord, the identity he had gained through living up to all the bad expectations that people had had of him, even before his birth; he had stopped pretending; his real self had encountered the living God.

Everyone who means real business with God, who is prepared to confess who he really is, and that he has cheated others of God's blessings, will find the Lord wrestling with that old nature and then coming in the power of the Holy Spirit to change him completely. God will not only cause us to own up to our false identity, and to the mess we have made of our lives, he will also completely change the sort of person we are. He will give us a new start and a new life to start with. He will give us a new name and a new power and authority. He will give us a vision of the Lord. We will become an 'Israel'. The new name means 'God rules' or 'ruling with God'. Is this new name going to be received by us now?

Israel – 'God rules'
How wonderfully Jacob was changed when he became Israel! The evidence of that change was seen throughout the rest of his life. After this dramatic encounter with God, Israel lived to have one more son. The

circumstances surrounding his birth were sad. Israel's wife was dying in childbirth but strong enough to say that their last son should be called 'Benoni', meaning 'the child of my sorrow'.

In the past, before transformation, Jacob had apparently been so apathetic that he had let his wife choose all the names of his children. Now, however, he was a new man: Israel. No longer indifferent to his family, he refused to let his last son be called 'Benoni'. He could remember how he had suffered far too much from his own nick-name, 'the cheat'. Having finally thrown off that terrible name through encountering the power of God, he was certainly not going to let his youngest son grow up with a negative appraisal such as he had suffered from. There were to be no more undermining conversations at home about the origin of names. His child was not going to be identified with the sorrow that surrounds death. Instead he would be Benjamin: 'the son of my right hand'.

The creeping rot in the family tree had been completely dealt with. Benjamin was spared the harmful conditioning which might have occurred but for the dramatic intervention of the Lord in Jacob's life. Instead, Jacob's son would face the future with an affirming name: one that would not have been appropriate for Jacob. Jacob's relationship with his father had always been bad; he had never been close to him; he had even wanted to deceive his dying father. But the grace of God had so transformed Israel that he could predict that his son would be very close to him – 'the son of my right hand'. There would be love and trust there.

The change in Israel was permanent. He no longer

blamed people or even God for what had gone wrong in
his life. He was so completely redeemed that he could
see the gracious activity of God through it all. Just
before he died, he blessed his grandsons with the
words:

> May the God whom my fathers Abraham and Isaac
>   served bless these boys!
> May God, who has led me to this very day, bless them!
> May the angel, who rescued me from all harm, bless
>   them!
> May my name and the name of my fathers Abraham and
>   Isaac live on through these boys! . . .
>   (Gen 48.15, 16, *Good News Bible*)

Israel could see the Lord leading him all through his
life – and his attitude to his deceased father was so
healed that he wanted the name of his father to live on
through his own grandsons.

What about us?

Can we identify in any way with Jacob and what
happened during his life? Do we covet someone else's
blessings? Jacob's attitude to Esau's blessing reflects
the attitude of those who see the way God blesses
someone else and want to be blessed in the same way,
rather than seeking the different blessing that Christ
has secured for them. Jacob typifies those who long to
be someone else rather than accepting who they are.

Are we set free from the mould others would press us
into? Have we been encouraged by family background,
nicknames, or stereotyping to be someone else? Have
we been torn between conflicting parental attitudes?
For many there is the constant struggle to live up to the
expectations of friends or associates. Having been

pressed into a mould that is harmful there arises a painful problem of identity.

Are we free to be the person God wants us to be? Often there is a conflict between what people expect of us and what God wants of us; between what has been programmed into us by our parents and what God wants to do with us. There is also sometimes a conflict between our own image of ourselves and how God sees us; between what we ourselves hope to be like and what God has decided. God is willing to do far more for us than we could ever desire but to do it in a way which is uniquely suited to our individual call and character. The Lord does not deal in duplicates.

God can break restricting moulds and set us and our children free. Destructive chains of cause-and-effect can be broken. As we have seen, Jacob refused to pass on to his child that stigma he had experienced. Defects need not be passed on to the next generation. Someone who has suffered from bad family relationships in childhood can be so transformed by the power of God that he becomes an ideal parent. But we must take responsibility for being who we are, and not blame others. Then we must confess who we are to the Lord, and let his dynamic power utterly transform us.

Statistically speaking, if we have come from a broken home, we are more likely to have a divorce. But we can be healed from our past and given stability and ex-pectations that will enable us to be life-long marriage partners. We may have emotional hang-ups which make us concerned about our effect on our families and friends. The Lord can undo the damage, purifying and freeing our emotions and giving us a new life.

What name do we live out? Are we a 'Jacob' or an

'Israel'? Are we someone who, through wanting to be someone else, robs others of the blessings God wanted them to receive through us? Or are we, like Israel, manifesting the effect of God's grace, his rule, his love and his power through our lives? We need to admit to ourselves and to God the name we secretly give ourselves. Do we think of ourselves as cheats, failures, faithless, powerless, useless, or even just ordinary? Are we 'actors' who *talk* much about God's dynamic power, but experience little of it ourselves?

When we *admit* and discard our old name, and as we live out our new name and begin ruling with God, we will stop inflicting unnecessary sorrow on others. We will refuse to see those given to us as Benonis; instead we will see them in positive terms. We will bless people, rather than take blessings away from them. We will be able to affirm people and, through the power of the Holy Spirit, we will be used to bring them into a new freedom so that they too experience the wonder of God's redeeming love and his gracious rule.

So God rules and our fullness of life in him will demonstrate this.

Chapter 6

A STRESSFUL HEART

'Why do I feel under stress? Surely as a *Christian* I should not be in that small minority who have stress-related disorders?' This common attitude only serves to increase the stress felt. It is perhaps valuable to notice straight away that people suffering stress are not in a small minority at all. All people suffer stress to some extent, and about sixty per cent of people attending GPs' surgeries in the United Kingdom are suffering from illnesses brought about by excessive stress. Half the hospital beds are occupied by people with more advanced stress-related conditions.

Their condition cannot simply be accounted for by their environment. They come from every section of society. About twenty per cent of all people in the United Kingdom will at some time in their lives have medical treatment for stress.

How do we deal with pressure or tension? How can we cope with the distress that is caused by all the demands that are made on our physical or mental energy?

Dr David Enoch, a leading psychiatrist, writes:

'Psychiatry has not, and never can, usurp the role of Christian faith. It does deal with man in great depth but, even after the most successful therapy, man can remain unhappy and unfulfilled unless his spiritual needs are met. He remains restless till he finds his peace in God and in God alone' (*Healing the Hurt Mind* p15). We need to be guided into the path of peace. This was the main aspect of the ministry of John the Baptist. He pointed people to Jesus and was called to show people that peace was like a path along which we must learn to walk. On this path we would experience forgiveness and grace (Lk 1.77–79).

The way of peace

To walk along this path of peace we need to realise first of all, that God is sovereign in our lives. Chaos is not the order of the day. We need to affirm that we have entrusted our lives to God, and that he is in control. As we continue to be dedicated to the Lord, he himself takes the responsibility for our lives.

We may sing quite often that God is almighty or proclaim that Jesus is Lord or call on the power of the Holy Spirit in our prayers. But our hearts may not be involved. It has been said that the longest journey is that from the head to the heart.

Many of us believe that there is something wrong about being anxious and under stress, as this following ditty implies:

Said the robin to the sparrow,
'I should really like to know
Why the anxious human beings
Rush about and worry so.'
Said the sparrow to the robin,

'Friend, I think that it must be,
That they have no heavenly Father
Such as cares for you and me.'

There is also Jesus' exhortation on the matter:

Do not worry about your life, what you will eat and drink;
or about your body, what you will wear. Is not life more
important than clothes? . . .
  For the pagans run after these things, and your
heavenly Father knows that you need them.
  But seek first his kingdom and his righteousness, and all
these things will be given to you as well.
  Therefore do not worry about tomorrow, for tomorrow
will worry about itself.
Each day has enough troubles of its own.

(Mt 6.25–34)

Sometimes we may find it difficult to believe that the
Lord of all creation, who takes infinite pains about the
details of his creation, really cares for us. It is one thing
to say with the apostle Paul, 'And we know that in all
things God works for the good of those who love him,
who have been called according to his purpose' (Rom
8.28). It is another thing so to *believe* it that our lives
display a peaceful resting in God's care and plan for
ourselves.

This experience of peace isn't something that we
arrive at once and for all. It is something that has to be
claimed time and again, and so in the early church the
Christians had to be encouraged to give way to the rule
of God's peace. Paul said, 'Let the peace of Christ rule
in your hearts, since as members of one body you were
called to peace' (Col 3.15).

This peace is not engaging in the ostrich-like activity of burying one's head and pretending there is no trouble in the world! It is taking into account that there is a sovereign Lord and that we have been reconciled to him and therefore we are living inside his kingdom of peace (Rom 5.1). We experience peace because peace has been *declared* and we have come to live in this new invisible reality.

Unfortunately some people don't realise that they can enjoy this peace. Some months after the second world war, soldiers were marooned on a desert island. Every time planes flew overhead they rushed for cover from the enemy. One day some troops landed and they hid in fear. Finally they were cornered and had to come out of hiding. The 'enemy' commander came towards them. They expected to be mown down by a round of bullets, but instead the commander stretched out his hand and said, 'I can see you don't realise that peace was declared months ago.'

The cross of Jesus Christ is God's peace declaration. That has happened whether we feel it has or not. The realistic response is to let the peace of God rule in our hearts, affecting our attitude to God, to people and to everything which happens to us. If we have peace with God, then we can have the assurance of his help and feel his strong protection. For this peace is not just a declaration of the end of war, or of neutrality; it means that God is actively 'for' us.

A landscape artist was wanting to paint a picture entitled 'Peace'. He went to the Lake District and marvelled at the beauty of the area and at the way the calm lake reflected the small white clouds moving across a perfect blue sky. But he felt that this did not depict peace as the Christian is called to experience it. A few days later he was at the seaside looking at the cliff face. There was a gale; the sea was pounding on the rocks; the rain was descending in torrents. In the cleft of a rock was a seagull, standing calm and still, sheltered from all the bad effects of the hostile elements and therefore not in a state of panic nor overcome by a strong desire to escape from the scene. The artist painted the latter to represent peace as the Christian knew it. We should be focused on God's power and not just on the size of the problem. Someone was once asked 'How are you?' to which the reply was given, 'I'm all right under the circumstances.' The Christian friend then remarked, 'You shouldn't be *under* the circumstances you should be *above* them.'

We must let the peace of God rule in our hearts. To do this we must face the reality of the cross, and the reality of God's love and power. We will sink only if we get distracted from focusing on him.

Don't be distracted

The apostle Peter saw Jesus walking on the water and wanted to walk towards him. He did so successfully at first. Then, still looking towards Jesus, he changed his focal length and saw the waves between Jesus and himself – and began to sink, but Jesus reached out quickly to save him (Mt 14.25–33).

Our focus should always be on Jesus – or we will be looking at the world in an unrealistic way; looking at it as if it were not subject to God's ultimate control. If we do not keep looking to Jesus then our problems will not only catch our eye but will appear to be large waves about to drown us. Our faith will be submerged and we

will begin to sink. Jesus himself is the one who creates
faith and sustains it within us – and therefore we should
be always looking to him.

> Let us fix our eyes on Jesus, the author and perfecter of our
> faith, who for the joy set before him endured the cross,
> scorning its shame, and sat down at the right hand of the
> throne of God. Consider him who endured such oppo-
> sition from sinful men, so that you will not grow weary
> and lose heart (Heb 12.2).

As we fix our eyes on Jesus we see in him an example of
someone who could trust God in all the cross-fire of
human opposition. He could entrust himself to God
when everyone was rejecting him. He trusted in God
even as he bled dying on the cross.

The early disciples were encouraged to see God's
sovereign power at work in their lives. They were sent
out by Jesus with a vision of his authority even over
death and therefore of the authority delegated to them
in all their future circumstances. He said 'All authority
in heaven and on earth has been given to me' (Mt
28.18) and, 'As the Father has sent me, I am sending
you' (Jn 20.21). They were to exercise authority over
all their circumstances, even if they drank poison or
were bitten by snakes. Paul realised this when he said 'I
can do all things through Christ who gives me strength'
(Phil 4.13).

We can learn to trust the Lord even for the unknown.
In our Christian pilgrimage, we may be asked by the
Lord to start something. We obey, only to find
ourselves completely bewildered by what transpires.
This bewilderment can bring stress to the point of
distress or be seen as a call to trust the Lord in the fog; to

say, 'I can't see a way through this but *he* can.' When I
was a child I loved a simple chorus which still lingers
with me now and is a means of reminding me of a great
truth. It goes:

> My Lord knows the way through the wilderness,
> All I have to do is to follow.
> Grace for today, strength for the way,
> And all that I need for tomorrow.
> My Lord knows the way through the wilderness,
> All I need to do is follow.

We do not need to know fully how things will turn out;
even less do we need to worry about things: what we *do*
need to know is that we are following the Lord.

Dealing with stress

In times of stress we may even lose our conscious
awareness of the Lord's presence with us. But the Lord
is still there. Sir Jacob Ashley prayed the following
prayer before the Battle of Edgehill: 'O Lord, Thou
knowest how busy we must be today; if we forget Thee,
do not Thou forget us. For Christ's sake. Amen.' Often
we are being placed in a position where we are being
strengthened by having simply to trust the Lord when
our feelings are numbed and we have no strength to
hang on to him.

Once when I was leading a mountain climbing
expedition in Snowdonia, a member of the party went
into severe panic. She was in no physical, emotional or
mental state to climb to safety. She was terrified that if
she moved she would slip on the scree and then fall to
her death over a cliff. Reaching down from a more
secure position, I was able to grasp her wrist. She was in
no state to grasp my hand, or contribute to her own

rescue, but I pulled her up to safety. She then experienced a mixture of emotions: including, obviously, relief, but also fear about what might have happened to her if she *had* slipped.

So often in times of bewildering stress, we add to the difficulty of our situation by believing that our well-being depends upon our firmly grasping the hand of God. The real truth is that at *those* times the Lord knows our weakness and inability to grasp his hand. He takes the initiative and grasps *our* hand firmly. Our confidence is not in our ability to hold on to God, but in God's ability to hold on to us. In the psalm David records his experience in these words:

> I waited patiently for the Lord;
> he turned to me and heard my cry.
> He lifted me out of the slimy pit,
> out of the mud and mire;
> he set my feet on a rock
> and gave me a firm place to stand.
> He put a new song in my mouth,
> a hymn of praise to our God.
> Many will see and fear
> and put their trust in the Lord (Ps 40.1–3).

The psalmist expresses his experience of deep despair which was brought on by stress. He then relates how the Lord lifted him up out of that despair.

Who's in control?

Excessive stress is often caused because we cannot see any constructive pattern in what is happening. Everything seems to be in utter chaos. If there were a clear cut enemy we would find it easier to fight. But in reality nothing seems that clear cut. Perhaps nothing seems clear at all. Do we, or do we not, believe in the Lord of all creation? Do we believe that the Lord created everything to fulfil his purposes, and that he hasn't let everything get out of control?

Our Bible begins with the words: 'In the beginning God created the heavens and the earth. Now the earth was formless and empty, darkness was over the surface of the deep.' We may say, 'Wait a minute. I cannot see God in that. He is the creator, but what do we find? There is only formlessness, emptiness, darkness everywhere! Are we saying that God created us to exist like that in chaos, emptiness, and darkness?' *No* – because the Bible goes on to say: 'and the Spirit of God was hovering over the waters. And God said, "Let there be light," and there was light.' Then he brought life and order and peace and harmony.

Wait in faith for the next thing God will do. Don't deny the stress of the present situation, but remember that the creator is *still* at work. The Spirit of God is still active and God is still saying, 'Let there be light.' Things are *not* out of control. Wait for the next step in *faith*. David learnt to do this: 'I waited patiently for the Lord; he turned to me and heard my cry. He lifted me out of the mud and mire; he set my feet on a rock and gave me a firm place to stand' (Ps 40.2). David's surroundings were depressing, but he focused on the Lord. If we just focus on the chaos, the darkness and the mire, we will panic and become very distressed, and never expect the Lord to rescue us miraculously.

The disciples had to learn this lesson.

Jesus said to them: 'Let us go over to the other side.' Leaving the crowd behind, they took him along, just as he was, in the boat. There were also other boats with him. A furious squall came up and the waves broke over the boat, so that it was nearly swamped. Jesus was in the stern, sleeping on a cushion. The disciples woke him and said to him, 'Teacher, don't you *care* if we drown?' He got up, rebuked the wind and said to the waves, 'Quiet! Be still.' [Greek says 'Be muzzled']. Then the wind died down and it was completely calm. He said to his disciples, 'Why are you so afraid? Do you still have no faith?' They were terrified and asked each other, 'Who is this? Even the wind and the waves obey him' (Mk 4.35–41).

Notice the fact here that the disciples were in the place of obedience. They were crossing the lake because Jesus told them to. The fact that someone is under stress does not necessarily indicate that they are being disobedient to God. Notice also how the disciples reduced Jesus to their own level in their thoughts. *They* were panicking, and so they were furious with Jesus for being calmly asleep as the boat appeared to be about to sink. At least he could have had the common decency to panic with them! Panic was the order of the day. They didn't ask Jesus for help; they were too busy being critical of his attitude. 'Don't you care Jesus? Don't you care?' Then Jesus spoke peace. He rebuked the disciples. They remained terrified, not now of the storm or the situation, but of having doubted Jesus' care and power.

If we are going to be afraid of anything, let us be afraid of underestimating the love that Jesus has for us and the power he has to deliver us, no matter what stressful situation we might find ourselves in.

Let us join with the psalmist and wait patiently upon the Lord, and in his time God will deliver us, and then like David, we will be able to say: 'He put a new song in my mouth, a hymn of praise to our God.'

Only commissioned work

Sometimes, however, we are in a state of stress as a result of doing some uncommissioned work. We are filling our lives with things that the Lord has *not* commissioned us to do. Jesus, by contrast, lived his life as a response to God's voice, and not as a frantic attempt to meet every need immediately. If Jesus had performed one more miracle, rather than passing by some of the people in need, he would have ceased to be perfect; consequently, he would never have saved anyone. Yet can *we* pass by people in need without feeling guilty? But if God tells us to help someone, then we should do so; and if he doesn't then we shouldn't accuse ourselves of being uncaring.

When Jesus visited the pool at Bethesda, he probably had to climb over many needy people in order to reach the one man whom he healed. Jesus was perfect, but he did not try to heal everyone there. He explained his actions later by saying he only did and said what his Father told him to say and do. Let us also do only what God tells us to do and stop trying to do everything or we will do nothing worthwhile. If it helps, ask a trusted Christian friend to pray with you and to discern both what God has called you *not* to do and what he has positively called you to do.

Throughout the year, but particularly at Christmastime, I receive literally hundreds of letters. Many are from charities. Some are duplicated prayer letters from strangers. I have had to learn to be very disciplined and to tear most of them up almost immediately, having decided before God about my giving and for whom, out of the thousand-and-one people, I will pray. I will not try to pray for every single person mentioned in all these prayer letters, because all my time would be spent reading prayer requests, leaving little time actually to pray for anyone!

The Bible records one occasion when Jesus saw crowds coming to meet him and deliberately escaped from them to go alone to a mountain to pray. He loved people sufficiently to get away from them at times. Only if he was refreshed by fellowship with his Father could he be of any use to them.

A famous contemporary man of prayer was given a tremendously powerful healing ministry from the Lord. People flocked to be prayed for by him. Sometimes you could see people queuing to be healed while he just continued playing tennis. He prayed for people in the morning and he knew that he owed it to the Lord and to himself to have time off in recreation. After playing tennis for a suitable length of time – he got back to praying for the sick again.

I once met a houseman in hospital who had been 'on call' for three days and nights. He was examining a patient. I sighed with relief when it became obvious that he didn't have to do anything for her, because he wasn't in a fit state to make himself a cup of coffee, let alone give medical treatment to a human being. The sister on duty masterfully escorted him out of the ward.

We are wrong in allowing ourselves to suffer from the stress that comes from trying to force ourselves into a mould that is unsuitable for us. The Lord has created you to be unique not to be a duplicate copy of someone else. Paul tells us, 'Do not conform any longer to the pattern of this world but be transformed by the renewing of your mind' (Rom 12.2). Don't be pressurised into doing things or thinking in a particular way just because that is the world's way. Don't let pressures control you but rather claim Jesus as Lord.

Live a day at a time. If I began the new year thinking that I would be required in the next few months to prepare some eighty different talks and sermons it would be enough to make me panic so much that I wouldn't be able to prepare one. Jesus said, 'Do not worry about tomorrow, for tomorrow will worry about itself. Each day has enough trouble of its own' (Mt 6.34).

Pastor Richard Wurmbrand was asked how he kept sane and, at times, even full of joy during so many years of solitary confinement, and how he endured so much interrogation and torture, without being crushed by the fear that he would crack up sooner or later. He replied, 'God does not give tomorrow's grace today. He will give that grace tomorrow. Today he will give grace for today.'

We have to learn to live each day at a time. We should not let unresolved problems whirl around in our mind, nor let our minds get into such a state that we cannot even think through the implications of something before another unresolved problem clamours for attention.

Part of the value of talking out our problems with Christian friends or ministers is so that they can help us to articulate the problem fully. When we have done that they can help us to present the fully faced problem to the Problem Solver. As we pray we know that Jesus will hear us. He will then address the storm, the hurricane or the mental whirlpool, saying to it, 'Be muzzled!' As people experience Jesus' power they may well start asking, 'Who is this?' Then, like those first disciples, they may realise that he is Jesus – someone so united to God that he believed in his sovereignty and therefore lived in his peace.

Unlike Jesus we are not perfect, and it doesn't help to condemn ourselves for imperfect reactions in life. But the Lord wants us to learn to express the sovereignty of God in our lives even when things look impossible. Sometimes I come across some situations which seem totally negative but God reminds me that he is the God of miracles. We should never take a fatalistic attitude to anything. God will intervene if he sees fit.

Let us avoid predicting what will happen merely on the basis of human calculations. Rather, let us trust the Lord's sovereign power. What were the odds on David and those on Goliath? David was a shepherd boy armed with a primitive sling. Goliath was a giant and wielded a heavy sword made specially for combat in war.

Think of Gideon. The odds were extremely low for him against the Midianites and he knew it. He was the youngest of the family. He was a member of the least important tribe. He belonged to a conquered people. Yet he was called by God to lead men into battle. The odds against him were made even more ridiculous when God reduced his thousands of men right down to 300, even before the battle started. Why did God choose Gideon and then reduce the number of his fighting men? It was to show, for everyone's benefit, that the battle and the consequent victory belonged to the Lord.

And what of the odds, humanly speaking, against one isolated and despised man on a cross outside Jerusalem on the first Good Friday having any impact whatsoever? But God can vindicate his own. God can bring resurrection. He can take people who, by faith, have been to the crucified and resurrected and ascended Lord. He can then pour upon them the Spirit of limitless power so that their crumbling lives, which were full of stress and defeat, can be transformed into lives that proclaim to those around them, 'Jesus is Lord. I am reigning with him.' Paul says:

> For though we live in the world, we do not wage war as the world does. The weapons we fight with are not the weapons of the world. On the contrary, they have divine power to demolish strongholds. We demolish arguments and every pretension that sets itself up against the knowledge of God, and we take captive every thought to make it obedient to Christ (2 Cor 10.3–5).

God has given us weapons of divine power which can demolish strongholds. The strongholds will not have the last word and defeat us. We will see the day-to-day relevance of being the children of the sovereign Lord. We can be disciplined in our thinking, making every thought captive to Christ. There is no good reason why they should always run wild. With our thoughts trained to be obedient to Christ and informed by God's Word, we can then limit ourselves to that part of the limitless work of Christ to which he has actually called us. No longer will we be defeated by the stress that comes from either showing no confidence in his sovereign control of our lives or from having our lives cluttered up with uncommissioned work.

Chapter 7

A WEAKENED HEART

What has made us the type of people we are today? To a large extent the answer is to be found in terms of our *reactions*. How have we reacted to our inherited nature? How have we reacted to our parents? How have we reacted to our circumstances, both while we were growing up, and in the present? How have we reacted to the love of God?

As we face these questions, it is helpful to realise that we are not isolated units but are partly the products of our reactions to our external circumstances. This is because the Lord did not create us so that we could be healthy and complete as solitary creatures. He created us to live in society. He himself declared: 'It is not good for man to be alone' (Gen 2.18); and he blessed Adam and Eve with the words: 'Be fruitful and increase in number' (Gen 1.28).

God's original intention was that we should be set within stable families, and be influenced by the nature inherited from parents. These relationships would display that man was created in the image of God. There are relationships within God's very nature. God, himself, lives as a Trinity-fellowship. Similarly, God wanted there to be a society on earth to reflect that fellowship in the diversity and unity of man and woman, and consequently in the social interactions of family life.

God's ideal

The unfallen relationships within a family were meant to reflect God's relationship to us. God's desire was for the succeeding generations to be brought up in the context of the family. The relationships within the family would represent the relationship between God and ourselves. The family would provide the context within which the revelation of God's nature could take place. The language which comes from our experience of receiving the love and discipline of a human father, would be used in the context of our relationship to God. Every father worthy of the name loves and disciplines his children. God is worthy of being called 'Father'. To receive discipline from God should not be interpreted as a sign of being rejected by him, but rather as a sign of his love.

> Do not lose heart when he rebukes you, because the Lord disciplines those he loves, and he punishes everyone he accepts as a son . . . Endure hardships as discipline; God is treating you as sons . . . God disciplines us for our good, that we may share in his holiness (Heb 12.5–10).

Often people start from their own human experience of family life and then decide what true fatherhood is like. But scripture says he must *start* with a revelation of true fatherhood as it is in God. Then allow our human understanding of fatherhood to be utterly transformed in order to conform to it. In reality the concept of fatherhood is actually *derived* from God's own nature, and is not a projection from our experiences of human fatherhood. Paul says he kneels 'before the Father, from whom all fatherhood in heaven and on earth derives its name' (Eph 3.14, 15, marg).

True motherhood, as well as true fatherhood, is to be found in God himself. The language surrounding our experience of deep but finite human love can be transformed into language concerning the nature of God. 'Can a mother forget the baby at her breast and have no compassion on the child she has borne? Though she may forget, I will not forget you' (Is 49.15).

Similarly, the relationship between Christ and his church should be reflected in the relationship of a *husband and wife* (Eph 5.22–33).

Brotherhood is also at the heart of Christ's relationship to us, and so the love that comes from God and transforms our life is bound to transform our attitudes to our Christian brothers and sisters; if it doesn't, we lie when we say we love God:

> We love because he first loved us. If anyone says, 'I love God,' yet hates his brother, he is a liar. For anyone who does not love his brother, whom he has seen, cannot love God, whom he has not seen (1 Jn 4.19–20).

The love which flows from living according to God's relationship to us is bound to be reflected in our relationship with others. It was God's intention in creation that our relationships within a family would reflect his relationship to us.

Distorted relationships

Our understanding of God's relationship to us is distorted. We live as part of a fallen world and our relationships are a distortion of God's relationship to us. Consequently we have a wrong understanding of relationships in general.

Such a distortion is easily illustrated from an experience of a young teenager. Immediately on becoming a Christian she was told to speak personally to God and call him 'Father' because he loved her. She refused to do so at first, because her own human father had been someone who came back home at night drunk and hit her mother. She would hide in the bedroom, completely terrified as she heard the shouting and screaming. It was a long time before she could use the word 'father' with any warmth of feeling towards God. Her understanding of fatherhood, based on her own human experiences, was completely distorted.

This may sound an extreme example but it is not all that rare. Fathers, mothers, husbands, wives, brothers and sisters do not live as God intended. They do not always demonstrate the revelation of God's love to us in their relationships.

Insufficient protection

Hearts are weakened through lack of protective love. We live in a world where there is a breakdown in the fundamental relationship between God and man, and this affects every human relationship. The most healthy relationships in which to live were those before the fall of Adam. Then there was total harmony between man and God and between Adam and Eve. But things are so different today and the family does not always provide the most healthy context for a child's development.

A parent should be able to gauge how much responsibility and freedom are good for a child as he matures.

Too much responsibility can harm a child but, on the other hand, if *no* demands are placed on him he can grow up to be weak and immature. The child will mature in a healthy way if the family relationships provide both security and the right level of demands.

As a result of the fall, rather than providing protection for children from too much stress, the family itself can be the *cause* of excessive stress. Much hidden misery often precedes divorces. Many parents act unjustly and selfishly. Sometimes the craving for a higher standard of material living means that children are left at a tender age for long hours outside the protecting love of the parents.

Among the saddest things I have come across is the sight of under-fives falling over and hurting themselves but not crying. The reason is that from an early age they haven't had anybody with a particular love for them; anybody on whom to pour out their tears. By the age of five some of them have begun to get 'hard' – no longer showing their suffering outside, but rather carrying it around inside themselves. Painful incidents where parental comfort has been lacking have an undesirable accumulative effect and leave an on-going weakness in the individual.

Imagine a boxer being cut by a blow. If he can get immediate treatment he will be able to return to the ring in a few weeks, with his face having completely healed. If, however, he returns before he has really recovered, then his opponent will not only reopen the wound, but also, possibly, leave the boxer with permanent weakness or disfigurement.

So many children carry inside them emotional wounds which have not healed and which have

permanent effects on their attitudes and emotions in
adult life.

To make matters worse, many people have been
taught that to be *adult* means to be independent and not
confess our weaknesses and our inner feelings. As a
result, long before reaching adulthood, many have
produced a protective mask which is always worn.
There is a desire to be treated as an adult in all respects
but the wounded child that has not been healed is still
there within. Such people project an unreal image of
themselves because they do not like to acknowledge
the person they really are. Are we in fact hiding ourselves from others? Do we wear a mask which is really
covering up our need to be healed within?

If such people, who were deprived of parental love,
have children, then their own children often reflect the
same characteristics. In a similar way, children who
have suffered from being in broken homes are far more
likely to have broken marriages themselves.

Over-protection
Some children are over-protected. This too is harmful
for their development. There must be a balance of
protection and demand in order for a child to grow up
into maturity and express this in adult relationships
with others. Otherwise he will become self-centred and
selfish, taking any criticism as a profound insult and,
frequently, bursting into tears or into bouts of rage.

We are the heirs of the imperfections of our parents;
we have been wounded as well as wounding ourselves.
The evidence of this is that we do not react as Jesus did
under pressure. Sometimes we react with a strength of
emotion which is out of all proportion to that which

provoked our response; or we find ourselves unable to
cope with certain demands or relationships. We may
express anger inappropriately or in the wrong way, or
damage ourselves by repressing it and, as a result, feel
a sense of guilt and condemnation or channel our
energies to self-justification.

So how can the weakened heart be restored? The
good news is that it occurs as the Holy Spirit miraculously enables us to enjoy our relationship with
God and uses the church to encourage us into this
enjoyment.

Relationship with God

First we must realise that we need our relationships
restored. This soon becomes apparent as we look at the
life and attitude of Jesus Christ, who must be the
measure of our maturity. He lived in a fallen world, in a
country which was full of every kind of stress. Moreover
he was frequently falsely accused and attacked because
of the hostility of his enemies. Often his closest friends
completely misunderstood the way he was thinking.
Nevertheless he never responded in hatred. He always
responded to others with the love of God; he never
responded according to people's attitude to him.

We often respond to people in an attitude that
shows that something in our past has left us weak and
vulnerable. In one area or another we are 'touchy'.

Secondly, we need to enjoy our relationship with
God. We can have new relationships without enjoying
them. I came across a young teenager whose father had
left her mother. Another man came to the home who
acted as her stepfather and a husband to her mother.
The girl liked her new 'father' but was only set free from

the fear that her real father would return and 'spoil everything' when her mother was officially remarried.

It is often helpful to look at the 'official' statements from the Bible which declare our new relationship to God; statements concerning the fact that when we received Jesus as Lord and Saviour, we entered into the reality of his death and resurrection (Rom 6.4): our old life was destroyed, and we were given a new start, and a new life (Jn 3.3; 2 Cor 5.17). We have no need to hide away behind a mask. We can enjoy being our new selves and being aware that the power of the Holy Spirit is inside us, giving us a new experience of inner strength (Eph 3.16).

Thirdly, we can experience the fruits of that relationship. We can be sure that we will be helped by a heavenly Father who will not allow us to experience too much stress. We can feel secure in the knowledge that he will never allow us to go through trials that are too great for us: 'God is faithful; he will not let you be tempted beyond what you can bear. But when you are tempted, he will also provide a way out so that you can stand up under it' (1 Cor 10.13). He will not let us be put in a situation that is so stressful that we have no alternative but to fall and be damaged.

The relationship between Jesus and his heavenly Father was always perfect and Jesus grew up perfectly. Secure in the relationship, he could face any kind of opposition. Often his human family misunderstood him; they even thought him to be mentally deranged on one occasion, but his security was in God's consistent love for him. To be healed, and to become like Jesus, we need to realise how secure we are in him. He said, 'My sheep listen to my voice; I know them, and they follow me. I give them eternal life, and they shall never perish; no-one can snatch them out of my hand. My Father, who has given them to me, is greater than all; no-one can snatch them out of my Father's hand. I and the Father are one' (Jn 10.27–29).

God protects, but he doesn't over-protect, because he knows that we will grow to maturity through facing conflict and not trying to avoid it.

He wants us to feel secure wherever we go, not just in a protected church-worship environment. The real test of our maturity is the way we speak and feel when we are in a hostile environment. Even for the infant Christian it is important to speak out what he inwardly believes. If he doesn't, he will not experience the reality of salvation. 'If you confess with your mouth, "Jesus is Lord", and believe in your heart that God raised him from the dead, you will be saved. For it is with your heart that you believe and are justified, and it is with the mouth that you confess and are saved' (Rom 10.9 –10).

Such confession both confirms faith and also takes people into situations which are not stress-free. In those situations, we must trust the Lord to help us but be prepared to fight for him as well, without complaining about getting wounded. It is as we fight that we mature, and learn to rely on God whatever the circumstances. 'If anyone acknowledges that Jesus is the Son of God, God lives in him and he in God. And so we know and *rely* on the love God has for us' (1 Jn 4.14, 15a). The stress involved in speaking out for Jesus as the Son of God, is balanced by the sense of security we have as we rely on him in the situation.

Church relationships

The weakened heart can be restored through mutual
encouragement in the shared life of the church. The
Lord has called the church into being to enable us to
mature by having the right support in a stressful world.
His own strength is often mediated through our fellow
believers in various ways.

Firstly, the Lord has appointed various ministries in
the church. These are to encourage the believers to
grow up together so that 'we all . . . become mature,
attaining to the whole fullness of Christ . . . We will no
longer be infants . . . Instead . . . we will in all things
grow up into him who is the head, that is, Christ' (Eph
4.13–15).

Secondly, we will be in a fellowship whose members
will *all* need healing. We can come to Christ directly or
in the company of fellow believers whom the Lord uses
to reveal to us where we need healing; for example, our
stunted emotional growth. We can then acknowledge
our need and pray for God's healing power through
which to grow into maturity.

Knowing that we are in a company of people all of
whom acknowledge their need, we can be encouraged
to admit our own pain, our wounds, our needs and
our weaknesses. In our attempts at self-protection, we
can try to hide our hurt but in the security of our
relationships in Christ we can stop hiding and be open
with one another. In the Body of Christ it is not a case of
those who are 'whole' healing those who are 'sick' but
the mutual ministry of the love of God between those
who are all in need of healing.

When we pray together, our own inner fear or hurt
will be shown to us. Sometimes the Spirit of God speaks

directly to us, and at other times he speaks indirectly to us through another child of the Spirit. Then we need to ask the Lord why we feel the way we do. We should not apply some method of inner groping, rather we should be looking to the Spirit to shed light and show what from the past is still crippling us, keeping us immature, or making us fearful in some area. As God makes us aware of things we follow Peter's exhortation: 'Cast all your anxiety on him because he cares for you' (1 Pet 5.7).

As we do these things, suppressed emotion might be released with tremendous force or we might start reliving something unpleasant, but there's no need to worry. The Lord will be putting healing oil on an area in our past which has remained unhealed and is still sore. Perhaps we were betrayed by someone, or left alone as a child to face some frightening experience. Whatever happened the situation can be 'relived' with God. In his presence we can face up to whatever it is that has haunted us over the years. Our fears will then lose their grasp on us; we will be set free.

Thirdly, we should face the need to forgive. If the hurt has been caused by what people have done to us, we will need to forgive them and allow no bitterness to remain in our hearts. We need to confess our sinfulness for harbouring resentment against those who mal-treated us. However justified our attitudes might appear in the light of human values, they are untenable in the light of God's love for us as sinners; a love that harbours no resentment against us for crucifying his Son.

We will need next to ask the Holy Spirit to fill us. Then, by the grace of God and to our surprise, we

will start desiring God's blessing on those whom, previously, we despised. We will be set free to obey the
exhortation that Paul gives: 'Get rid of all bitterness,
rage and anger, brawling and slander, along with all
malice. Be kind and compassionate to one another,
forgiving each other, just as in Christ God forgave you'
(Eph 4.31–32). The fact that we will be able to pray for
God's blessing on those people will give us encouraging
evidence of the dynamic power of God's love living
within us and changing us. We will also need to receive
the power of the Holy Spirit to heal and restore.

So, acknowledging all the weaknesses that we have
inherited and released from all the damage that our
response to our environment has caused over the years,
we will be free to receive the Lord's forgiveness and
love; free to forgive others; free to love others as Christ
forgives and loves us; free to relate to others in a
wholesome way within the Body of Christ. As this
becomes our new experience day by day, then the Spirit
will work within us in order to make us mature, until we
reach the full maturity of Christ himself.

Chapter 8

A FEARFUL HEART

What makes us laugh? A variety of things. The right sort of laughter can be very relaxing for us and beneficial. But there is a type of laughter that reveals an inner fear. Two parents once called their son 'He laughs', or 'Isaac'. It is interesting to discover what this choice of name shows about the character of those parents.

Afraid to believe

Abraham was told by God that his wife would have a change of name. Her name would no longer be Sarai but Sarah. This was because God would bless her and she would bear Abraham a son (Gen 17.15–18). On hearing this news Abraham 'fell face down: he laughed, and said to himself, "Will a son be born to a man a hundred years old? Will Sarah bear a child at the age of ninety?"'

There was a conflict between Abraham's outward appearance and inward feelings. He instinctively fell face down in an act of humility before God, acknowledging his greatness. This was the way he wanted to appear because this was the way he wanted to be. But the inner reality was so different.

Within Abraham there was an involuntary unbelief caused by a fear of all the suffering that would follow disappointment. Many long years had led him and Sarah to despair of ever having a child. This fear expressed itself in what appeared to be scornful laughter on hearing the promise of God. Abraham could see that God could bless Ishmael. He even suggested to God that that was the best thing to do in the circumstances, because for Sarai to have a son was beyond belief.

You might be able to identify with Abraham in his laughter of unbelief. God had to repeat the promise before Abraham evinced a different attitude. The New Testament writers have insights into this event which would be difficult to deduce from Genesis: 'By faith Abraham . . . was enabled to become a father because he considered him faithful who had made the promise' (Heb 11.11).

Initially Abraham had had faith about his future offspring (Gen 15.6; Rom 4.3, 22) but after the delay he had to hear the promise stated twice before he became firm in faith again.

Some while later Sarah joined in the laughter. Her particular type of laughter came from a heart full of fearful scepticism. She had known for years the disappointment of not having a child. She had been mocked about her childlessness. It was a very sensitive and painful subject to her. When three visitors came to her tent and she overheard one of them saying that she would have a son, she laughed sceptically (Gen 18.10). Though she was hidden in the tent, and laughed in her heart only, the Lord knew about it. Nothing is hidden from him. He searches the secret thoughts of our hearts. He knows about our hidden scepticism. He also knows that we, like Sarah, are so ashamed of our scepticism, that we will not face it, or admit it to him. 'The Lord said to Abraham, "Why did Sarah laugh and say 'Will I really have a child, now that I am old?' Is anything too hard for the Lord? . . ." Sarah was afraid, so she lied and said, "I did not laugh." But he said, "Yes, you did laugh"' (Gen 18.13–14).

Sarah could see the hard realities of her situation but not the reality of the Lord's power. She could only remark on how old she was. The Hebrew word used for 'old' here is the one used of a garment that is worn out and falling to pieces. It is just when we are 'worn out' that we lose hope. But the Lord takes us in our worn-out state and performs miracles through us. Confess to the Lord any sceptical thoughts and any involuntary laughter at his promises. Sometimes we are in such a state that fear of disappointment may lead us to believe that God's promises apply to everyone else but they most certainly do not apply to us. We cannot hide from the Lord and imagine that our attitude is not seen by him. Confess your unbelief to the Lord and ask him to replace it with faith.

The word of the Lord is sure. Sarah laughed at it; nevertheless it was to be fulfilled in due time. 'The Lord was gracious to Sarah as he had said, and the Lord did for Sarah what he had promised' (Gen 21.1). Sarah gave birth to a son and Abraham called him 'Isaac'.

Laughter of a different type was predicted when Sarah said that everyone who would hear what had happened would laugh with her: the laughter of joy that *follows* when a promise is fulfilled before your very eyes or the Lord has acted miraculously. What a great deal of joy we forfeit in the Christian life if we are full of fear and scepticism about what the Lord has said. We might even feel guilty as we try to hide our unbelief from God. God always fulfils his promises, as we realise to our joy in the end, but how different the time of waiting will have been for those struggling with their scepticism than for those confidently expecting him to act! The latter will have experienced much joy during their wait.

Dealing with fears

Fear has to be cured if joy is to last. There can be a deep fear in people which they have never faced, and until they do face it and find healing they will never have lasting joy. Many Christians have been to places where the Lord has been blessing his people, and from which they returned feeling wonderfully joyful. But it does not last; it cannot because fear cannot be removed by joy. New joy just puts a veneer over inner fear.

The fear that made Sarah sceptical about the promises of God had to be dealt with. It was the fear of God's blessings being snatched away from her that made her bitter towards Hagar, to whom Ishmael had been born while she had been childless. This fear generated harsh feelings towards another whom she felt had succeeded where she had failed and included anxiety over *never* being fulfilled in life. With all these fears, it was hardly surprising that she couldn't relate positively to others.

When Sarah had a son, we might expect her to have been full of joy. But if that joy was to be lasting, she would need to be healed from fear. Though all her hopes seemed to be attained, she was afraid that the blessings promised by the Lord would be snatched away from her son. So she became fearful when she saw Ishmael playing with, or perhaps mocking, Isaac. She then wanted Hagar and Ishmael to be expelled from the family home. Though her circumstances changed completely, she still had no lasting joy because the inner condition which she had had for a number of years had not been healed. She had never admitted, either to herself or to the Lord, that she had a fearful heart. She needed to admit her ingrained fears before the Lord would heal her.

We, too, have to come to the Lord, recognising that we have ingrained fears and bringing with us our past hurts. Then the Lord will deal with our fearful hearts and heal us.

There are good grounds for having faith in God: after all, he is sovereign. It is irrational to fear that his promises will not be fulfilled. Rational fears are very valuable if they make us behave in sensible ways that protect our lives, such as refusing to pick up a red-hot poker or to cross a very busy main road or motorway blindfolded and alone. In these instances, our previous experience of hot pokers or dangerous roads rightly affects our behaviour in the present. But sometimes we have fears that are totally irrelevant to our present circumstances and only impede sensible behaviour. In fact, such fears might be detrimental to our wellbeing. For example, a terrible experience might make someone so afraid that they dare not leave their home to go outdoors.

When we come to the promises of God, we often bring the irrational fear that tells us that these promises will not be fulfilled. Our experience of life tells us that people, time and again, either deliberately or unintentionally, make promises that they cannot or will not fulfil. We then, irrationally, treat God as though he were a fallible human being by questioning the reliability of *his* promises. It was Sarah's irrational fear that showed itself in the way she laughed and prevented her from joyfully anticipating the fulfilment of God's word. She should have trusted what God said to her.

We can have confidence in the word of the Lord. Isaac was born . . . 'as God had said' and as 'God had promised', and 'at the very time God had promised' (Gen 21.1–3). God *always* keeps his word. He has the *power* to do what he says he will do. He also has the power to redeem the mess that results from our unbelief, our unhealed past condition, and our present mistakes. I find this encouraging. Time and again, I would be afraid of doing things in case I made a mess of them, but for my belief in a Redeemer, who can redeem my mistakes.

Sarah hurt people as a result of having a fearful heart. Abraham wanted to keep Hagar and Ishmael in the family circle, and we might have expected that the Lord would have sided with Abraham against Sarah's desires to be rid of them; after all, her attitudes sprang from jealousy and fear. But blessing and salvation are achieved as God's plan is fulfilled. Isaac was chosen for a special purpose; nevertheless God reassured Abraham that Hagar's circumstances would be redeemed, her son would prosper and be the founder of a great nation.

With this reassurance Abraham obeys at once. He got up early next morning, and sent Hagar and Ishmael away with provisions for the journey. They went to the wilderness near Beersheba in the south. When their provisions ran out, in despair Hagar placed Ishmael under the shade of a tree to die. These two people were victims of Sarah's harboured fears. But God who is sovereign, spoke to Hagar in her despair: 'What is the matter, Hagar? Do not be afraid' (Gen 21.17). The Lord knew all about their need and their circumstances before he asked the question, but it was necessary for Hagar to unburden her heart to him. The Lord then promised that Ishmael would be greatly blessed and would found a great nation; he also met their urgent need, by opening Hagar's eyes to see a well. Her eyes were also opened to see the sovereignty of God: he would redeem all the mess that had resulted from Sarah's fears. The story of Abraham and Sarah is an encouragement to step out in faith, rather than hold back in fear and disobedience.

Fear of looking ridiculous

Another reason for holding back might be pride which shows itself in a fear of being made to look ridiculous. We can read of how the Lord brought to Naaman healing from such a fear (2 Kg 5.2–14). He was a leader among men, a great commander of the Syrian army who had won many notable victories. The king of Syria held him in high esteem and, when Naaman contracted leprosy, sent him with a letter of recommendation to Israel's king to seek for healing. The king referred him to Elisha the prophet of the Lord.

Naaman was a proud man. He had, no doubt, worked hard to build up a reputation for himself and was prepared to guard it zealously. One of the worst things that a proud person can imagine is to be put in a place where he is made to look small and insignificant.

Naaman delighted in impressing people. When he arrived somewhere, he arrived in style. He stopped outside Elisha's house with his chariots containing 750 pounds (345 kg) of silver and 150 pounds (70 kg) of gold and ten sets of clothing. To Naaman's horror and disgust Elisha didn't come out to see him. Elisha was not impressed by outward appearance, much to Naaman's annoyance.

The prophet sent a message that Naaman was to go and wash in the Jordan seven times and then his flesh would be restored and he would be made clean. Naaman's personal pride was hurt. He also felt he had received an affront to his national pride. He represented a great country; he had fought for Syria with great success. He was known everywhere as a Syrian national hero. 'Go and wash in the Jordan!' He must have thought to himself, 'Why, that pathetic river is little better than a stream when compared with the majestically flowing rivers of Syria.' But nobody stands any taller by standing on his dignity.

The reality was that God and Elisha simply saw him as a leper, in need of the same healing as anyone else in that condition, and treated him accordingly. The fact that he was a leader of men was neither here nor there. The important thing was his need to be cleansed from leprosy.

Whoever we are, each one of us needs to be cleansed from the leprous marks of sin, and the only cure for us, whoever we are, is the blood of Jesus spilt on the cross: 'The message of the cross is foolishness to those who are perishing' (1 Cor 1.18a). Whatever our standing in society, and however proud or fearful we are, we all need to repent and receive cleansing and a new start.

Naaman needed to swallow his pride and be submerged in the Jordan, no matter who was there watching him. In fact, he got angry, and wanted to go home, but his servant persuaded him to go to the river. He went down into the water, self-consciously aware of people watching him, once, twice, three times . . . After the seventh time 'his flesh was restored and became clean like a young boy' (2 Kg 5.14). He was totally and utterly healed.

Let us be encouraged to reject the pride and disobedience that originates in fear and unbelief and come in humility, faith and joy to receive cleansing, healing and the power of the Holy Spirit. Then we can walk in newness of life to God's glory.

Fear of the past

Some people are gripped by a fear of the past. Their past disappointments prevent them from seeing the possibilities of the present.

One evening two men walked out of the city of Jerusalem towards the small village of Emmaus. They were downhearted as a result of following a leader who had failed in all their expectations of him. A third man joined them (Lk 24.13–35). He asked them, 'What are you discussing together as you walk along?' They must have thought, 'How insensitive of him to pry into our private grief!' Impatiently Cleopas asked if the stranger were the only person in Jerusalem who did not know the things that had happened recently. 'What things,' the stranger asked, and they explained to him about Jesus and the cross, and about some women who were adding to their confusion with their talk about Jesus having risen.

The irony was, of course, that *Jesus* was the stranger. What had caused them grief had been experienced at a far greater level by him. He explained to them from the Scriptures why he had to die for them. They arrived at Emmaus and recognised him as he broke the bread, saying the same words that he had said at the Last Supper with them. He then vanished.

But notice what the two people did next. They *returned* to Jerusalem. They went back to the place of betrayal and disappointment. They returned to face those from whom they had been running away. They were now unafraid of being followers of someone whom many thought of as having failed in his mission. They were no longer ashamed of their crucified Lord. He, too, was not ashamed to be associated with them. He had met them after their failure to remain loyal to him during the hour when he stood in great need of friendship. He had met them in their hour of despair. They were restored by meeting him and trusting him as their resurrected Master. They went back to the place of previous failure where they had let Jesus down and where he could deal with their fears.

They met behind closed doors, locked by fear of persecution. This proved no barrier to the risen Lord, who entered and said, 'Peace to you,' and added, 'As the Father sent me, so I send you.' The Father had sent Jesus to proclaim fearlessly and boldly the love of God and the power of his kingdom. The disciples had their thinking changed, as they came to realise that Jesus had given his life to this work, even to his last breath.

They returned to Jerusalem where Jesus had died for

them, and where they would experience the outpouring of the Holy Spirit on their lives on the day of Pentecost.

If we have a 'Jerusalem', we must not run away from it. We have to return to that place so that our irrational fears can be faced and so that we can be healed and made strong, if we are to know lasting joy. We have to return to the place of previous failure and unbelief, and even to the place of sceptical laughter. We have to return to the place where our pride was so hurt that we turned our back on it and walked away saying we would never be found there again. We have to allow ourselves to become vulnerable again rather than clamming up in our self-protective shell.

In short, we have to return with all our fears to the place of the cross where God fulfilled all his promises. At the cross our irrational fears of being disappointed by God will be dealt with by divine grace. In the cross we will see that his sovereign plan was fulfilled as Jesus died so that our sins might be forgiven, and that God's perfect plan for our life can *still* be fulfilled. If we return, then Jesus will cleanse and heal us. More than that, he can redeem the chaos we have created around us.

When we have returned to our Jerusalem and found Jesus there also, he will submerge us in his forgiveness and in the love and power of the Holy Spirit, and through his power set us free from all fear and from pride, to serve the Lord with joy. We will hear the Lord say again: 'I will rejoice over Jerusalem and take delight in my people; the sound of weeping and of crying will be heard in it no more' (Is 65.19).

Chapter 9

A CONSECRATED HEART

When we pray for the sick we need to be conscious of the active presence of the Lord with his people. 'Is any one of you sick? He should call the elders of the church to pray over him and anoint him with oil in the name of the Lord. And the prayer offered in faith will make the sick person well; the Lord will raise him up' (Jas 5.14, 15a). The person who is ill is to be active in taking the initiative and calling for the elders. They are to pray and anoint the sick person with oil. The oil represents the fact that the believers are going to give the person in need all necessary help and support; it also represents the fact that the Lord himself will be active in raising up the sick person. The connection is made explicit in the Old Testament.

Oil and consecration
Oil was used when the Lord was consecrating his people or setting them apart for himself and for his use, so making them holy to himself. The Lord told Moses to make anointing oil and then go and 'anoint Aaron and his sons and consecrate them so they may serve me as

priests' (Ex 30.30). They were to be consecrated to serve as priests. The kings were also consecrated or set aside for their particular task: 'Then Samuel took a flask of oil and poured it on Saul's head and kissed him saying, "Has not the Lord annointed you leader over his inheritance?"' (1 Sam 10.1).

So we see that the priests were anointed to offer worship and service to the Lord and to declare what God had done for his people; and the kings were anointed to rule with authority and to be protected from their enemies.

The apostle Peter writing to Christians said: 'You are a chosen race, a royal priesthood, a holy nation, a people belonging to God, that you may declare the praises of him who called you out of darkness into his wonderful light' (1 Pet 2.9). So we are anointed to be kings and priests to worship the Lord, to serve him, and to rule by his power. What a tragedy if we were not consecrated to the Lord and not alert to what he is saying to his people and to his desire to lead them on in the power of his Spirit!

Jesus told a parable of ten virgins (Mt 25.1–13), five of whom ran out of oil so that when the bridegroom arrived they were no longer in attendance. They represent people who have stopped looking for the activity of the Lord and who are found unprepared when he comes. They had 'oil' to begin with but their consecration fell away. We as God's people are a royal priesthood consecrated to the Lord as priests and kings.

The people who lived during Jesus' visible earthly ministry not only consecrated the living with oil, but they also anointed the dead with oil. It was thought that death was the final leaving behind of all possible distractions from being fully dedicated to the service of God and to worshipping him. There is no desire to compromise in heaven!

An utterly amazing incident is recorded in the life of Jesus. He was anointed for burial while he was still alive! Imagine that friends had invited an honoured guest to their home for a meal today. As they are eating the undertaker comes into the room and starts measuring up the honoured guest for a coffin. If you had been that honoured guest, how would this have affected your appetite for eating? But we read: 'Now when Jesus was at Bethany in the house of Simon the Leper, a woman came up to him with an alabaster flask of very expensive ointment, and she poured it on his head, as he sat at table' (Mt 26.6). And Jesus explained (v11): 'In pouring this ointment on my body she has done it to prepare me for burial.'

The anointing was a wonderful reminder to Jesus that he was always completely consecrated to God his Father. What a wonderful thing, if, when we are about to die, we were to be reminded that we are already consecrated to God: that we were already set apart for him both now and in eternity. Anointing with oil spoke of such consecration to the Lord.

Oil and healing

Oil also spoke of God's power to heal. There are many things that cause us to suffer ill-health and to feel sick; we can be bruised and left hurting or damaged in the spiritual, mental, emotional and physical aspects of our nature. The oil of God can heal such bruises. People anointed with the Holy Spirit can be restored.

At one time, Israel of old was in a bad condition as a

nation. As a people they had rebelled against God, and consequently the health of the nation was in a terrible condition. Isaiah says of these rebellious people, 'Your whole head is injured, your whole heart afflicted. From the sole of your foot to the top of your head there is no soundness – only wounds and welts and open sores, not cleansed or bandaged or soothed with oil' (Is 1.5–6).

Oil, as well as representing the activity of God consecrating his people to himself, was used as a *healing agent*. The nation rebelling against the Lord had no oil. They continued in an unhealed state because of their opposition to God and his means of blessing. In everyday life oil was placed on wounds and bruises as a healing agent. Even when sheep bruised their heads the shepherds used to rub oil onto the bruise: 'The Lord is my shepherd . . . You anoint my head with oil' (Ps 23.1, 5).

Oil was also used as a natural cure by the good Samaritan in Jesus' parable. 'He went to him and bandaged his wounds, pouring on oil and wine' (Lk 10.34).

The Lord wants his people to be healthy: he wants to anoint them with oil for their healing, and he wants his people to become the agents of his healing power to others. When Jesus sent out his disciples we are told that 'they went out and preached that people should repent. They drove out many demons and anointed many sick people with oil and healed them' (Mk 6.12–13). This was to continue as long as there was a community of faith with elders (Jas 5.14).

Oil and empowering

So we see that oil was used to *consecrate* and *heal* God's people. But God's people also need to be *empowered* to live for him.

There are ways by which God's people can forfeit God's power and so be powerless. One of these is through deliberate sin in thought, word or deed. If we are clinging on to some sinful habit or attitude then we have to be prepared to reject that, *before* we can know God's power in our lives. We must, initially, be *willing* to reject and renounce the sin.

This truth is clearly shown in the Old Testament sacrificial system (Lev 5.11–13). It was clearly stated that no oil was to be used in a sin offering. Sin had to be dealt with first: it had to be renounced and repented of before one could ask for anointing and empowering. God's restoring power is kept from people by their deliberate sin.

Unloving, jealous attitudes are expressions of sin. If we harbour these attitudes towards someone, then we cannot ask at the same time to have the power of the Lord fully expressed in our lives. The reason for this is clear: the power of God is supremely the demonstration of his practical love to us. His power is a love-motivated expression of his being: it expresses his loving desire to set us free. He wants us to be free from the suffering that comes through being oppressed by the evil one or by demons; free from the pain caused by our own failure or by our mental or physical condition. If we want the gifts of God to be manifested powerfully in our lives, we should pray that we be full of love to God and also to each other.

In the Old Testament there is a sacrifice called a jealousy offering, which was to be offered by someone into whom the spirit of jealousy had entered. Perhaps jealousy of other people's lives or ministries is one of the most damaging things among believers even today. In Old Testament times, the jealous person had to come to the tabernacle and make a sacrifice, but he was strictly commanded not to use oil in his sacrifice and in his offerings to the Lord (Num 5.15). Why was this? It was because jealousy indicates an absence of the power of the Holy Spirit. Our own experiences in life may well illustrate this truth.

So God requires that we turn away from sinful habits and attitudes, including an unloving, jealous spirit. He wants to see us obeying and loving him and his people. When he sees this, he will give us what we otherwise could not receive: the oil – or, in other words, the power of the Holy Spirit. The apostle Peter speaks of the Holy Spirit as he 'whom God has given to those who obey him' (Ac 6.32b).

The oil used for anointing was olive oil. This was produced by grinding the olives to pulp and squeezing out the oil. A famous place for the growing of olive trees and the production of olive oil was the Mount of Olives just outside Jerusalem. At the foot of the mountain was a garden which contained olive presses. The Hebrew for 'olive-press' is 'Gethsemane'. Jesus went to Gethsemane and to the crushing agony of prayer there, so that his disciples, who at that time were so weak that they couldn't even pray with him, might be anointed with olive oil – *consecrated* to do God's will. They were to be healed and also be given the ministry of healing. They were to be empowered and made strong so that they could declare fearlessly the deeds of him who had delivered them out of the realm of darkness and into his glorious light.

The pioneer of our faith, the Lord Jesus, went via Gethsemane to Calvary and then to resurrection and ascension, so that from his ascended position he could pour out the oil, namely, the power of the Holy Spirit at Pentecost. This was so that we could know the reality of the health-giving power of the Spirit in our lives. Jesus was called 'the Christ' which means 'the anointed one', but as such, he is the *anointing* one. He anoints others with the power he exercised himself. He lived in the power of the Holy Spirit. Only the anointed could anoint others. Only Jesus Christ can pour out the power and love of God into our lives. He is the only High Priest who can anoint us to be a kingdom of priests and a royal priesthood.

Cleansed, consecrated and empowered

This ministry of Jesus is wonderfully foreshadowed in the Old Testament in the ceremony for the cleansing of the leper (Lev 14). The leper had to come to the door of the Tabernacle (v24), bringing with him a lamb for a guilt offering and also a container of oil. Then the priest would kill the lamb and place some of the blood of the guilt offering on the tip of the man's right ear, symbolising cleansing from the wrong things that he had wilfully listened to; on the thumb of the right hand, symbolising cleansing from the wrong things he had done; and on the big toe of the right foot, symbolising cleansing from the effect of the wrong places to which he had gone.

After this was done (v26) *oil* would be poured into the priest's own left hand and he would consecrate the oil to the Lord's use. He would place some on the leper's right ear to consecrate it and signify that he would no longer wilfully listen to evil; some on the thumb of his right hand to consecrate him and separate him from doing unholy things, and some on the big toe of his right foot to consecrate him and separate him from going to unholy places.

The leper would thus be completely cleansed by, and completely consecrated to, God. But that was not all. There was an all-important third part to the ceremony. The first two parts, wonderful though they were, were not sufficient (v29). The rest of the oil in the palm of the priest's left hand would be poured on the leper's head for his empowering. Cleansed and consecrated, he also needed to be empowered by the outpouring of the Spirit (v30). The leper would respond by giving a thank-offering to the Lord. He would express thanks for three things: that his sins were forgiven; that he was consecrated to the Lord, and that God had promised to empower him.

Jesus our great High Priest with his own blood will touch our ear, our hand and our foot, so that we can be totally cleansed from the leprosy of sin. He has made it possible for ear, hand and foot – all of us – to be totally consecrated to him, so that we hear his word to us, do what he tells us, and go wherever he wants us to. More than that, he pours out the power of the Holy Spirit upon us so that we might be empowered to live as he lived on earth. By giving us his power he makes us whole and healthy and enables us to pray for others that they also might experience the healing power of God. It only remains for us to live lives which are a sacrifice of open thankfulness to the Lord for all he has done for us.

Healing and thankfulness

Thankfulness is very important for our healing. This is illustrated by the story of the ten lepers whom Jesus met as he travelled along the border between Samaria and Galilee. He was about to enter a village. As lepers were regarded in every way as 'unclean', they did not come near Jesus but rather called to him, 'Jesus, Master, have pity on us!' (Lk 17.13). Jesus called back to them saying that they should go and show themselves to the priests. The priests had the duties of medics, and part of their job-description was to give a clean bill of health to a leper who was healed before he could resume his place in society. It is significant that as the lepers were on their way to the priests they were healed; not as they stood still but as they acted in obedience to the word of Jesus.

But only *one* came back praising God. He, as it were, made his thank-offering to God (Lev 14.31) by throwing himself at Jesus' feet and thanking him. The other nine lepers did not return and it was to this thankful man alone that Jesus said 'Arise, go thy way: thy faith hath made thee whole' (Lk 17.19, AV). All the lepers had been physically cured – but only one was declared whole: only one was seen to be well on all levels. If someone is not thankful then they are not as healthy as they could be.

We should be overwhelmed with a sense of gratitude that Christ has called us and that we have received his strength and grace (1 Tim 2.1). Like the psalmist we will be *seen* to be whole if we are thankful; we will know his power and glory as we worship him, lifting up our hands in praise and saying, 'Because your love is better than life, my lips will glorify you'

(Ps 63.1–5). We will be thankful, satisfied and anointed people of the Lord. We will have consecrated hearts.

Chapter 10

AN ANXIOUS HEART

(Healing from anxiety about healing!)

One of Britain's leading surgeons specialising in heart and lung transplants was asked how he selected the most suitable people for the operation. He said that he chose people who really enjoyed living rather than those who just wanted to avoid dying. His experience had proved to him that the former category of people stood a far greater chance of recovery from the operation than the latter. His conclusions, based solely on empirical observation, were that the joy of living encourages healing and the fear of dying discourages it.

When we are ill it is important not to be anxious about the fact that we are not well. Sometimes our responsibilities make it difficult for us to relax because our mind is invaded by hundreds of things that need to be done. But more serious than that, however, is the self-condemnation that often occurs. It is easy to become anxious about the very fact that we are ill at all. If this is so, we need to hear Paul's exhortation to the Philippians: 'Do not be anxious about anything, but by prayer and petition, with thanksgiving, present your request to God. And the peace of God, which transcends all understanding, will guard your hearts and your minds in Christ Jesus' (Phil 4.6–7).

Anxiety about the relationship between sin and illness

One cause of anxiety may be the fact of the illness itself. Some people feel morally guilty about being ill and personally responsible for their condition. Of course, some people *have* sinned against their bodies and minds and this *has* resulted in their suffering. Others, however, bear no personal responsibility for their condition. The whole creation is fallen. The corporate sin of society affects the well-being of all its members. Bad housing may be an example of how the sins of the fathers can be visited upon the children to the third and fourth generation (Ex 20.5). Another may be family pressures over which the sufferer has no control. We may be ill through what other people do to us.

So though illness is caused by sin, it may not be that of the individual concerned but that of another or of society. Whatever the cause, the main point of healing is to bring forgiveness of sin and freedom from guilt to the afflicted person.

If it *is* the individual's own sin which is primarily responsible for his condition, he needs to be encouraged to confess his sin and receive forgiveness. After doing this sincerely, he needs to be encouraged to accept the absolute nature of God's forgiveness. It is beyond human understanding how an all-knowing God can forget something! Evidently, however, he can wipe his memory banks clean when it comes to our confessed sin. He declares, 'I will forgive their wickedness and will remember their sins no more' (Jer 31.34b). The prophet Micah asks the Lord, 'Who is a God like you, who pardons sin and forgives the transgression . . . You will again have compassion on us; you will tread our sins underfoot and hurl all our iniquities into the depths of the sea' (Mic 7.18, 19). Corrie ten Boom would have us add: 'And then he erects a sign saying "No fishing".' When the Lord forgives, he forgets.

What is true for us individually is equally true for us corporately. God forgives and heals us corporately if we repent of our sins: 'If my people, who are called by my name, will humble themselves and pray and seek my face and turn from their wicked ways, then I will hear from heaven and will forgive their sin and will heal their land' (2 Chr 7.14). This healing comes through the forgiveness which is offered us as a result of the atoning work of Christ on the cross.

On one occasion, Jesus was asked if a particular man was born blind because of his own sin or that of his parents. But he made it clear that neither the blind man nor his parents' sin was the cause. He then turned the conversation from the area of blaming people to the higher plane of bringing glory to God. We are born into a fallen world full of physical imperfections and everyone suffers as a result. It is good to recognise this and not be over zealous in attributing sickness glibly to the sin of the individual sufferer.

Anxiety about faith

Another cause of anxiety has to do with faith. Some are anxious that their lack of faith has made their healing unattainable. There is a 'name it and claim it' school of thought. These Christians believe that whatever we require, including good health, can be demanded

from God. This philosophy is dangerous because it is
bound to lead people to conclude that if only they
had sufficient faith, they would be immune from all
ailments.

It is true that Jesus encouraged people to have faith
in him for their healing. It is also true that where there
was unbelief he was restricted in the number of powerful works that he could accomplish (Mt 13.58). Most
healings which Jesus performed were in the context of
faith. But that faith was not always expressed by the
person needing to be healed. When men brought to
Jesus a paralytic, lying on a mat we are told:

'When Jesus saw *their* faith, he said to the paralytic,
"Take heart, son; your sins are forgiven"' (Mt 9.2).
It was the faith of the men carrying the paralytic which
was noticed by Jesus. If there is lack of faith when
someone is being prayed for, then those praying for the
sick should first search their *own* hearts. They should
not add to the misery of those who are sick by making
them feel guilty of unbelief.

Moreover it should be recognised that it is the
normal condition of a Christian to have faith in God. If
someone is showing unbelief, then that person is
fighting against his God-given relationship of trust in
God. Faith is not something that has to be created by
us; still less is it something to be 'worked up'. The
believer has been born again into a relationship of trust
in God and is aware of the Holy Spirit calling out from
within, 'Abba, Father.'

If the Spirit of him who raised Jesus from the dead is living
in you, he who raised Christ from the dead will also give
life to your mortal bodies through his Spirit, who lives in
you . . . you did not receive a spirit that makes you a slave

to fear, but you received the Spirit of sonship. And by him we cry, 'Abba, Father.' The Spirit himself testifies with our spirit that we are God's children . . . if indeed we share in his sufferings (Rom 8.11–17).

It follows that it is against our new relationship with God not to have faith in him; we would be actively opposing the influence of God in our lives. When Jesus could do no mighty works because of people's unbelief, the people were actively opposing his claim to be a prophet speaking on God's behalf. Jesus himself could do little in the way of healing for people who actively rejected everything for which he stands. It is clear that few, if any, Christians stand in that category. We must look elsewhere, other than their supposed lack of faith, in trying to understand why some believers are not healed.

It cannot be stressed too much that faith in God is the normal attitude of a child of God towards his Father. It is a gift of God to his children. It is not something that we can work up as if it were a human attribute that needed to be stirred into action by our own efforts. Neither is it something that depends upon atmosphere.

Jesus promised his disciples that where two or three are gathered in his name he would be there with them (Mt 18.20). He said this to make it clear that large numbers are not required; his power can be manifested where there are only two or three. In fact, where there are large crowds of Christians, it is often more difficult to distinguish between psychological factors and what Christ is doing for those who are simply placing faith in him for healing. Large crowds do not produce faith; it is a gift from God.

By-passed by God?

A third cause for anxiety centres round the fact that some are healed and others are not. Those who are not may feel that they have been by-passed by God. The example of Bartimaeus may be helpful here. He was anxious that Jesus should not pass him by (Mk 10.46–52). He had heard that Jesus was going to pass through Jericho, so he sat by the roadside and shouted and shouted, 'Son of David, have mercy on me!' Jesus called him over and asked him what he wanted. (Often Jesus wants us to be very explicit indeed and say openly what we desire.) The blind man said, 'Rabbi, I want to see.' Jesus said, 'Your faith has healed you.' Immediately he saw and followed Jesus.

Here was a man who would not be put off by people who thought that he was not a worthy case for the attention of Jesus. He persisted in faith. He would not let this opportunity of a lifetime slip through his fingers.

Jesus did not by-pass people just because they were regarded by society, or even by themselves, as unworthy of his ministry. On a previous journey through Jericho, he had stopped under a sycamore-fig tree and called to the outcast tax-collector Zacchaeus to come down. He wanted to have a meal in that man's house that day. The people, not least Zacchaeus, were amazed at Jesus's choice of company. Sitting opposite Jesus eating his meal, the tax-collector must have felt that Jesus was reading him like a book. At last he blurted out that he would repay handsomely everyone he had defrauded in the past. A healing had taken place in Zacchaeus' mind and sense of values. Jesus commented, 'Today salvation has come to this house.' His host had shown faith in God and was thus acting as

a son of Abraham. The lost had been found
(Lk 19.1–10).

Even in his last moments on the cross Jesus did not
ignore those in need. The thief on the cross next to him,
who at first mocked, but then became aware of the
perfection of Jesus, was not rejected by him. The man
turned in faith to Jesus and asked for pardon, and
was immediately given it and the assurance of Jesus'
protecting presence beyond death.

We need never be afraid of being rejected by Jesus if
we are penitent and exercise the faith that God gives to
all his children. After all, Jesus came because the sick
need a physician, not those who are well! (Lk 5.31–32).

Anxiety in waiting

One of the most difficult things to do is to wait upon
God's timing. How hard it is to be patient and trust his
sovereign ordering of our lives! If we are in need of
healing, we sometimes have to ask the question, 'Is
right now the time Jesus is going to heal me or is he
going to do something else in my life first of all?'

How difficult it must have been for that man who sat
daily at one of the gates of the Temple in Jerusalem. He
had been there every day for years. Jesus must have
passed him by on each occasion that he went through
that gate to the Temple to pray and worship. Jesus
was the famous healer. He was known to have raised
Lazarus from the dead and, as a result of that, great
crowds had followed him. But he did nothing to heal
this cripple. That man must have felt unloved and
by-passed by Jesus. But the reality was so different.
After Jesus' crucifixion, resurrection and ascension, the
man *was* healed by him. One day he called out to Peter

and John for money, as he did to all the passers-by. Peter told him that he didn't have any money, then said: 'In the name of Jesus Christ of Nazareth, walk.' At this, the man leapt to his feet and praised the Lord. He had not even been asked to exercise faith!

This incident reminds us of the importance of God's timing in healing. We should never anxiously ask the question, 'Does God want to heal me?' because the answer is so obviously, 'Yes'. The final state of all Christians will be one of total wholeness. In heaven we will all find ourselves to be fully healed. Then there will be 'no more pain, for the old order of things has passed away' (Rev 21.4). In heaven we see the full will of God for his children completely fulfilled. So, according to the Bible, we should never doubt God's desire to heal us. But we may well ask, 'Is God going to heal me *now*?' The man at the Temple had the painful experience of seeing Jesus the healer walk past him time and again as he had to wait upon God's perfect timing. But at the right time, he was given perfect health or 'complete healing' (Ac 3.15).

No doubt Timothy would have liked instant healing from his stomach trouble and his frequent ailments, but his condition persisted. He must have been prayed for by the church and possibly by Paul himself, but he wasn't healed of his persistent illness. Notice how Paul responded to Timothy in this matter. He didn't exhort him to have more faith so that a miracle could take place! Instead he gave him good advice about how to *live* with his physical weaknesses (1 Tim 5.23).

Paul knew what it was like to live with a 'thorn in the flesh' which would not go away (2 Cor 12.7–10). In all probability this 'thorn in the flesh' was not an illness:

the word 'thorn' is only used elsewhere in the Bible of external attacks on people and so here Paul might have been referring to persecution (*Cf.* Num 33.55; Jos 23.13; Jud 2.3). Moreover, Paul talks of his resolve to delight 'in insults, in hardships, in persecutions, in difficulties', but never says he delights 'in illnesses'.

It is relevant to note, too, that Paul expected to be set free from something which he found very exhausting. Surely, he must have thought that he could spend his energies in a better way than coping with, and feeling weakened and drained by, this 'unnecessary' trial. He *expected* the Lord to do something about it, *until* the Lord told him otherwise.

If we were to apply this same approach to healing, would we find that we had to change some of our presuppositions about prayer for healing? Often we don't expect to be healed *unless* God dramatically tells us we are going to be healed! Paul prayed until the Lord stopped him praying in that way. Similarly, we should pray and expect to be healed unless the Lord assures us that our healing will not take place this side of the grave. When the Lord speaks like that to us, we need have no anxiety about remaining unhealed.

Anxiety and dishonesty

When people are anxious about healing, dishonesty can sometimes creep in. Some may know that they have received some measure of healing but be anxious about the fact that they have not been totally healed. As a result, they may pretend that they are better than they actually are. This pretending is saying to the Lord, 'My unreal world is better than the real world in which you work.'

It is often more difficult to be honest about our lack of
healing if we are surrounded by people who have shown
faith in Jesus and have been healed. This may have
been the case for the blind man of Bethsaida who wasn't
instantly healed by Jesus. This man would have had
every reason to *expect* such healing from Jesus, who was
spending such a high proportion of his time healing
others. People were seeing the Old Testament proph-
ecies fulfilled (Mt 11.3–6; Lk 4.16–21). The age of the
Messiah had come and people knew what to expect:
'Then will the eyes of the blind be opened and the ears
of the deaf unstopped. Then will the lame leap like a
deer, and the tongue of the dumb shout for joy' (Is 35.5,
6), and 'The Spirit of the Sovereign Lord is on me,
because the Lord has anointed me to preach good news
to the poor. He has sent me to bind up the broken-
hearted, to proclaim freedom for the captives and
release for the prisoners, to proclaim the year of the
Lord's favour' (Is 61.1).

In the context of all that, imagine yourself as the
blind man. How would you have felt if Jesus himself
had taken you by the hand, led you outside the village,
spat on your eyes, laid his hands on you, and then said
'Do you see anything?' Would you have pretended that
your sight was totally restored and so gone away only
partially healed? The blind man didn't lie; he was
relaxed enough to tell Jesus the truth. He said, 'I see
people; they look like trees walking around.' The man's
sight was still impaired and he told Jesus so, and Jesus
put his hands on the man's eyes and his sight was
totally restored: he saw everything clearly (Mk 8.22
–26). How good that the man was not so anxious to be
healed that he said to himself, 'I *have* been healed "in

faith". I claim my healing although some of the symptoms remain the same.' There was no double thinking with this man. He was honest enough to tell Jesus to his face that he had not done a perfect job in healing him! He was not too anxious to say that. He trusted Jesus enough to be honest with him so Jesus brought about the second stage in the man's healing.

We should not be so anxious to see immediate results that we fail to be honest with ourselves or with our Lord. If the Lord has begun a healing work within us, whether it be physical, mental, spiritual, or emotional, we need to acknowledge thankfully what he has done but keep praying for more and more healing and keep coming to Jesus until we are sure he has completed the work he has begun in us.

Focus on Jesus

Miraculous healing comes from looking directly to Jesus himself. It is often good to have someone praying alongside you as you seek the Lord for healing. However, this situation is full of dangers. It is all too easy to rely on the company of the other person to such a point that your prayer-partner starts being regarded by you as a special 'go-between' between you and God. Some involved in the healing ministry, and especially in the counselling aspects of the healing ministry, place themselves in the position of mediators of grace between the person and the Lord, thus usurping his place and creating a dependency upon themselves which is detrimental to lasting healing. 'For there is one God and one mediator between God and men, the man Christ Jesus' (1 Tim 2.5).

It is interesting to notice how Jesus communicated

with people such as the blind man just mentioned. He used many means to focus that man's attention on *himself*. The man was blind, so he was deprived of the faith-inspiring sight of seeing Jesus. But Jesus compensated for this by using the man's sense of touch and of hearing. He first grasped the man's hand and walked with him some distance outside the village where he had met him. The man then felt the spittle and Jesus' hands on his eyes. He heard Jesus' question. Finally, he again felt Jesus' hands placed on his eyes. In these varied ways, Jesus was communicating his own presence to this man and making him aware that he, himself, was actually doing something to heal him. This evoked the man's faith in the person of Jesus. No doubt Jesus could have prayed a silent prayer and the man could have been healed but far better for the man to learn that wholeness comes from a positive trust in Jesus as one's life is focused on him.

By dealing directly with Jesus we have our faith built up by him. Think of the leper who was uncertain about Jesus' willingness to heal him. He tentatively knelt in front of him and said, 'Lord, if you are willing, you can make me clean.' Jesus then did two things. He stretched out his hand and touched the leper. The untouchable had been touched – and by Jesus of all people! Holy people especially were expected to avoid the unclean. But Jesus was unashamed to associate with the man: he was unafraid of losing his own holiness, knowing that the holiness of God was not something that had to be protected from contamination but so powerful that it could conquer the results of evil in the world. The death of Jesus was later to prove the point once and for all. But here Jesus, having established his willingness to heal the leper by touching him, reinforces his actions with the simple words, 'I am willing. Be clean' (Mt 8.2–3).

There need be no fear that Jesus will completely forget us and ignore our condition. As we call to him, he will draw near to us in order to impress on us his loving concern for us (Ps 50.15).

How much faith do we need?

Sadly, sometimes, we can find ourselves concerned about the *amount* of faith we have. We are anxious about this, rather than forgetting about ourselves and looking directly to Jesus and focusing on the one who creates and perfects faith. It is wrong for us to put our faith in the amount of faith we have, rather than simply looking to Jesus for healing. As we look to him, we will find that faith comes as a by-product. We will have it without all the futile anxious activity of trying to create it.

After an evening service during which people were invited to stay behind if they wanted prayer for healing, I met a man who had travelled with his family to the service with that purpose. His eyes had become badly mis-shaped and he was losing all sight through them. I asked him if he had faith that Jesus would heal him there and then, and he confessed, in rather an anxious way, that he did not know if Jesus would do anything for him. I found myself saying, 'Don't worry about that, because *I* believe that Jesus is going to heal you, now.' The man forgot about his own spiritual condition. He lost all anxiety about his faith, and the Lord healed him. The Lord had spoken to me so that I could say something to divert the man's attention away from his anxiety about having enough faith, and be fully focused on Jesus himself.

In the teaching of Jesus, he is far more concerned about where our faith is focused, than about our being confident that we have massive faith. If we want to see immense obstacles removed, all we need is to have faith as small as a grain of mustard seed. That seed is so small that it is difficult to see it with the naked eye. Jesus said: 'I tell you the truth, if you have faith as small as a mustard seed, you can say to this mountain, "Move from here to there" and it will move. Nothing will be impossible for you' (Mt 17.20). Our task is not anxiously to measure our faith but to look to the creator of all real faith – himself. 'Let us fix our eyes on Jesus, the author and perfecter of our faith' (Heb 12.2).

So, to conclude, we should not be anxious. We should not automatically believe that our illness or our 'lack of faith' are things we should feel guilty about. Nor should we feel by-passed by God if, unlike others, we are not instantly healed. Instead we should wait patiently on his timing. He wants us to be honest with him, not pretending that we are feeling better than we are. Above all, the Lord Jesus wants us to cast aside all our anxiety, and simply look to him: all things are possible, with him; he loves us with an everlasting love and takes every opportunity to demonstrate his love for us.

Chapter 11

AN UNSURE HEART

In the previous chapter we saw that anxiety about being healed can itself harm our health and well-being. We saw that we should believe that God wants to heal everyone and this desire in God's heart will be fulfilled for his people as they arrive in heaven for eternity.

But must we always have an unsure heart about healing? Can we today have firm, well-founded confidence that we are definitely going to be healed? If so, how does the Lord instil that certainty in us?

We see that it is not just a case of having faith in God's nature. There was no lack of faith exercised by Paul and Epaphroditus and Trophimus who had temporary illnesses (Gal 4.13–14; Phil. 2.27; 2 Tim 4.20). Timothy is not blamed for having a long-term illness. He is never exhorted to repent of his sins so that he could have real faith and so that every barrier to his being healed could be removed. There were times in Jesus' ministry when he healed everyone of all kinds of sickness and disease (Mt 4.23); when those who touched him were healed (Mk 6.56); when all who were oppressed by the devil were set free (Jn 10.38). There were other times when he just selected certain individuals and concentrated on healing them only.

Many blind or lame or paralysed people were at the Pool of Bethesda when Jesus just singled out one individual for healing (Jn 5.1–9). That person was not chosen because of his faith. He had become resigned to the fact that he would never be cured after thirty-eight years (v5). The circumstances were all against a miraculous cure for him (7b). When asked by Jesus if he wanted to be cured, he avoided answering the question which had become so painful. He had given up. Jesus was asking a genuine question. Sometimes we prefer the security of staying as we are, even if things are not as they should be, to having our lives turned upside-down by a miracle.

The paralysed man made the mistake of telling Jesus, of all people, that there was nobody around to help him. Have we ever done that? Have we told the Lord of all creation, when he speaks to us about our condition, that there is nobody there who can help us? Are we too spiritually blind to realise the potential of a situation in which the Lord is present? At Bethesda, Jesus took the initiative out of the hands of the man at the pool-side. He had displayed no faith whatsoever, yet Jesus said to him, 'Get up! Pick up your mat and walk.' And, before the man could recover from the surprise, he had got up and started walking.

At the Pool of Bethesda Jesus had singled out one man among many and healed him. This man had showed no faith; his condition was directly related to his sinfulness, yet he didn't come to Jesus in a penitential frame of mind. He had to be warned to stop sinning (v14). Why was he singled out for healing and not any

of the others? It was because God the Father had told
Jesus to meet that particular man and to heal him; and
he had not spoken to Jesus in the same way about the
other sick people there.

When Jesus was questioned about the healing he
said, 'I tell you the truth, the Son can do nothing of
himself; he can do only what he sees his Father doing,
because whatever the Father does the Son also does'
(Jn 5.19). Evidently Jesus had seen that God the Father
was about to heal this particular person, and that he
himself was called to be an instrument of that healing.
This directing of ministry by God the Father is reflected
in the believers' use of the gift of the word of knowledge.

Word of knowledge

It is significant that today the Lord has restored the
'word of knowledge' ministry in the context of praying
for people to be healed. Instead of leaving us to guess
what is about to happen the Lord takes the initiative
and tells us beforehand what he is about to do, so that
we can be instruments of his will. He directs us to
particular individuals. He informs us of the particular
area in a person's total being that he is about to touch
with his healing power. In this way we can approach
the right people at the right time and in the right way.
Sometimes we mis-hear the Lord and make mistakes.
But if we do hear him clearly we might, for example, be
asked by someone to pray for physical healing, but
experience the Lord revealing that this will only occur
after some emotional problem has been dealt with. Or it
might be the case that healing would only be retained if
the person were to change his attitudes and behaviour
(Jn 5.14c).

Words of knowledge are given to us as we listen to the Lord. It is often a good practice to pause in silence before praying for someone and ask the Lord to give us the right line of approach. It is important to listen to what he says to us, and not just rush in relying on the way the individual has diagnosed his own need. Often the inner cause of sickness is hidden from the person concerned. The insight usually comes in the form of a mental picture or in words or by physical sensation. If insight is given and declared, it strengthens the faith of all concerned. Those praying and being ministered to become aware that God is already active in the situation. This helps to remove the negative thoughts and fears that nothing will happen or that God will have to be persuaded of the reasonableness of this particular request for healing. When God uses this means to enlighten and raise faith 'the prayer of faith' will bring healing (Jas 5.15).

God should be seen as sovereign in healing. Our prayers will not bring about healing. Prayer is not effective in itself. The only point of praying is that God has chosen to act in the context of our praying. It is not our prayers but God's response to them that brings healing to people. This healing takes place through a meeting of the individual with God's power and not as the result of a religious exercise which is effective in itself.

God's timing
This word of knowledge ministry, in which God shows what he is going to do next, must be exercised in the context of a clear belief about God's general intentions for healing humanity. It is clear that God originally

created the world with the intention that its inhabitants should be fully healthy. Then sin entered the world and imperfection marred the whole of creation. The whole creation now groans with pain as it awaits the final day of its restored perfection (Rom 8.22). Yet that day is already dawning. The power of the age to come – God's power – has already entered this world through the death of Christ on the cross. He has brought about the means of our forgiveness and poured out upon us the blessings of his kingdom. 'Surely he took up our infirmities and carried our sorrows . . . by his wounds we are healed' (Is 53.4–5; cf Mt 8.16–17). Peter takes this up and applies it to physical healing: 'He himself bore our sins in his body on the tree, so that we might die to sins and live for righteousness; by his wounds you have been healed' (1 Pet 2.24). Moreover Jesus has removed from us the fear of death by his resurrection (1 Cor 15.56, 57).

The Lord has dealt with all the obstacles which might prevent his healing power from coming into our lives; with the sin which is the barrier that stops his healing grace coming to us. For the Christian there is nothing 'wrong' with being sick. We can relax and await God's timing, knowing that we have already been reconciled to God through the death of his Son (Rom 5.10; Col 1.21, 22); we can joyfully proclaim, 'Jesus is Lord', while waiting for the power of the world to come to invade our lives.

I once took some of my theological students to the Dorothy Kerrin Home of Healing at Burrswood. Here science and Christian faith work together in complete harmony. A woman there had been bedridden for many years: she was paralysed and could hardly move her body at all. Volunteers were asked to go and visit her, but the students were reluctant – afraid of what they might see and of their inability to cope with it. But they went, and when I saw them afterwards, they were amazed. One of them said, 'We entered her room and the whole place seemed to be filled with the peace and glory of God. *We* travel hundreds of miles each year but that woman is living in a far bigger world than we are!' She had learnt how to wait upon the Lord's timing. Spiritually, she was strong. Quietly and peacefully, she trusted her Lord. Her very being was expressing what the Psalmist wrote: 'I am still confident of this: I will see the goodness of the Lord in the land of the living. Wait for the Lord; be strong and take heart and wait for the Lord' (Ps 27.13, 14).

We need to distinguish between what God has undertaken to do *immediately* for all who enter into a covenant relationship with him and what – albeit also the fruit of the cross and resurrection – is not guaranteed to everyone immediately.

In the former category are the forgiveness of sins, the new birth, eternal life, unity with Christ and the reality of the indwelling Spirit as guide. In the latter category are those things that are inessential to our eternal salvation but which God wants his people to enjoy here and/or in eternity. These include the gifts of the Spirit and total healing on all levels. Christians are exhorted to 'eagerly desire the spiritual gifts' (1 Cor 14.1); they are not automatically given as part of the package-deal of being a Christian. We are to seek for healing from the Lord because physical health, although one of the results of the atonement, is not a necessary and automatic result. Lack of healing therefore is no indication of the absence of unity with Christ or of a faithless attitude towards God. If we are not immediately healed it is good to ask why this is so. The Lord may give us a word of knowledge which reveals why he is telling us to wait awhile for our healing.

Sometimes we see someone healed in a matter of minutes; at other times it takes longer. Colyn, a student at Keele University, came to the vicarage and expressed his concern about his rapidly deteriorating eyesight. We talked for a while. My wife afterwards asked why I hadn't prayed with him. Although the thought had gone through my mind, I gave it no serious consideration for I had no word of knowledge to pray with him then. The next morning he came to my office and *asked* for prayer. That was the Lord's chosen time. We went into the university chapel and prayed and he was healed there and then. He looked into the mirror and literally could hardly believe his eyes. They were completely healed. Meeting him over a year later, he pulled my leg about my having to wear glasses when *he* had not had to wear any since the day we prayed!

Colyn's story

I received this letter from Colyn ten years after the healing:

> Like many students at university in their final year, I found that the amount of work needed to be completed before finals began to resemble the picture of putting a quart into a pint pot. So I spent far more time reading and writing in that year than I seemed to in earlier years. The pace quickened after the Christmas vacation and by the time that finals approached, my body decided that it had had enough. About a fortnight before exams were due to

start, my eyes became so strained that I could no longer read and write. Trying to focus on the text of any book was painfully frustrating and as the days passed I became both concerned and acutely aware that time was running short without any improvement in the situation. I consulted a doctor and optician and was provided with salve and spectacles. This helped but did not halt the discomfort. I remained longsighted and uncomfortable with the close work necessary for revision and writing.

I remember reading in James' letter that the sick should ask the elders of the church to pray, so I shared my difficulty firstly in a general way for prayer and then the next day was bold enough to ask point-blank for prayer for healing.

I remember nothing of the words which were prayed, but I do remember the results. We were together in the small chapel which was open for prayer during the day. I listened to Don praying and added my own thoughts silently and waited. I was not long in waiting. I quickly felt refreshed and light, as if I had taken off a heavy rucksack. Joy filled me as if it was in my bloodstream filling every part. I could see clearly again without the frustration of the past few days. The joy continued to well up in me and I literally leapt for joy, touching the low beam of the chapel near the entrance – just like a footballer scoring a goal! Glorious is the only word which can even partially describe how I felt.

I later discovered that I had also been healed of a minor stomach complaint that I had learnt to live with.

Colyn's healing was instantaneous, but sometimes one has to pray for a longer time. This is what Francis MacNutt calls 'soaking prayer'. It is too easy to give up praying when nothing dramatic happens at once. Instead of doing something completely supernatural sometimes the Lord answers our prayer by speeding up the 'natural' agents of healing that he built into our being when he created us. Or he may want to take us through various stages and levels of healing, making us aware of the significance of each. It may be necessary for us to know what there is about us that needs healing before we are actually healed. Also, Jesus taught us that it is needful sometimes to persist in prayer and not give up if we do not receive the answer immediately. The important thing is that, in the end, our prayers will be granted as we ask in his name (Lk 11.5–10). We should be open to a word of knowledge from the Lord that enables us to know what he is going to do and his order of doing things.

A time to die

There may be times when we should refrain from praying for someone's physical healing. I am sometimes called to the bedside of someone who is dying. How should we pray in those situations? Quite clearly there is no 'rule of thumb' approach to be applied to all such circumstances. One has to rely on the guidance of the Holy Spirit in our approach to people who are seriously ill and in sharing any specific words of knowledge. The first thing to discern is whether or not it is the Lord's time for the person to leave this world. He gives us life here on earth and takes it away. Our times are in his hands (Job 1.21; Ps 31.14, 15a). It is pointless praying for someone to be renewed in the body if their God-appointed time to die has arrived. We should, rather, pray for that person to continue to trust the Lord until his or her last breath. We should also pray for those soon to be bereaved.

Francis MacNutt writes: 'Whenever we speak of healing, I think we must also think (and maybe speak) of death, because death is the ultimate healing.' I believe that it would be more accurate to think of death as the gate we pass through in order to enter the state of perfect healing by the resurrection. But he is right in saying that Christians should not fear death or be afraid of speaking about it and preparing people for it.

Similarly the human body usually 'runs down' towards the end of one's stay on earth. There are, however, notable exceptions: Caleb who was just as strong and vigorous in battle at the age of eighty-five as he was at the age of forty (Jos 14.10, 11). The natural ageing process slows us down so that we have more time to contemplate and prepare for death. To some people death is a terrifying vacuum and they look for more meaning behind it. If we already trust the Saviour who has died and been raised, then we also realise that he is the 'first-fruits of those who have fallen asleep' (1 Cor 15.20) and see death in a different light: as the gateway to our going home to be with Christ whom we already know as a compassionate Friend.

I used to visit a dear old lady in a geriatric ward. Every week she would greet me from her bed with the words, 'I want to go home'. By this she meant that she was impatient to die; she wanted to see her Lord. She didn't understand much about the after-life, but she knew all she needed to know: that she would be with Jesus. Her obvious delight at the possibility of dying caused a real dilemma for the nursing staff who felt that they had a duty to encourage her to fight to keep death at a distance. In the circumstances, they were at a loss to know what to say to her.

To have a right attitude to death involves having eternal life. Only then can you rejoice in Christ's victory over death, and realise that you are included in that victory. The fear that clouds our thinking is removed as we know that, even in this life, we have a foretaste of eternal life in heaven. Often the unbeliever sees sickness as a foretaste of dreaded death itself. Such people always fear sickness, and the thought that their life is ebbing away brings great panic. These very attitudes of mind, in themselves, reduce the quality of life. You cannot be fully alive if you fear death. Christians have a different perspective on death, and therefore on health. 'If only for this life we have hope in Christ, we are to be pitied more than all men' (1 Cor 15.19).

Sometimes people are 'struck down' before old age by a terminal illness. As such a person looks to the Lord with confidence, he prepares them in their remaining days on earth for their life with him in eternity. Sometimes the rush of life here on earth distracts us from fully enjoying our relationship with God himself. David Watson declares in his book *Fear No Evil* how the Lord showed him in his last few days of physical weakness and immobility that all of David's ministry meant 'absolutely *nothing* compared to *his* love-relationship with him' (p171). With that preparation David faced death with serenity and without fear.

Life in all its fullness

But apart, perhaps, from having a positive attitude

towards ageing and death, we don't always demonstrate the truth that Jesus came to this world so that we
might have life in all its fullness (Jn 10.10). Our
expectation of what the Lord is going to do for us is
pathetically low most of the time. We close our minds to
words of knowledge. We decide what is going to happen
inevitably. But as we read of the thirty-three occasions
in which Jesus completely healed those who were
chronically sick, we should, at least, open our minds to
the fact that the risen and ascended Lord, 'is able to do
immeasurably more than all we ask or imagine, according to the power that is at work within us' (Eph
3.20–21).

We need to call upon the Spirit's help so that we
might have greater expectation of healings today, since
no eye has seen, no ear has heard, no mind has con-
ceived what God has prepared for those who love him –
but God has revealed it to us by his Spirit. 'The Spirit
searches all things, even the deep things of God' (1 Cor
2.9, 10). Then we will hear the Spirit give us words of
knowledge about any particular ailment, so that we can
claim those healing benefits of the atonement that do
not come to believers automatically but are given so
that we might enjoy the fullness of life here and now.

Chapter 12

A HEART OF FAITH

What is the relationship between healing and faith? We are often encouraged to have more faith if we want to be healed. It is clear that at or after some healings Jesus said, 'According to your faith it shall be to you,' or, 'Your faith has made you well.' But *what is faith?* Often it is spoken of today as if it were man's contribution to his healing; as if it were some spiritual attribute we can decide to exercise at will. Speakers on the subject of healing often try to create an 'atmosphere of faith' by the use of music or certain mesmerising songs. So what is it?

What is faith?
In the Old Testament the word 'faith' only occurs once (Deut 32.20), though a word derived from it is also used once (Hab 2.4). Dr Leon Morris writes, 'This does not, however, mean that faith is unimportant in the Old Testament, for the idea, if not the word, is frequent. It is usually expressed by verbs such as "believe", "trust" or "hope", and such abound' (*The New Bible Dictionary*). To have faith in God is to have a right attitude

towards him. The psalmist describes the right attitude:
'Trust in the Lord, and do good . . . Delight yourself in
the Lord and he will give you the desires of your heart.
Commit your way to the Lord; trust in him and he will
do this' (Ps 37.3–5). The psalm continues to mention
the blessings we will receive if we do trust God and live
by faith in him.

This attitude is sometimes described in terms of
trusting the Word of God because of its origin in the
mind of God (Ps 119.42). Throughout the Old Testament, the focal point of our faith is in God himself. We
are encouraged to 'trust in the Lord with all your heart
and lean not on your own understanding' (Prov 3.5).
In seeking healing we must trust God and not be put off
by our own lack of understanding or even by our
spiritual or emotional condition (Prov 28.26; Ezek
33.13). This trust in the Lord must not be usurped by
any human being not even a doctor. No one has the
right to promote himself as the source of healing (Jer
17.5; 2 Chr 16.12).

By contrast, in the New Testament, the words for
'faith' or 'faithful' occur 307 times! The great theme of
the New Testament is that Christ has come. He has
died and has been raised. As a result of this, if we have
faith or trust in what Jesus did on the cross, rather than
in man's own abilities, we can receive salvation (Jn
3.16).

This faith in Jesus is to be expressed by trusting
certain things that he said about himself (Jn 8.45, 46).
It is never enough to believe a truth *about* Jesus. Faith
involves a refocusing of one's whole life. It is trusting
him in a way that is bound to be expressed in one's
behaviour (*cf* Jas 2.18). This faith takes someone *into*

Christ (Jn 15.4). By contrast, without faith it is impossible to please God (Heb 11.6). It is by faith that we are focused on the invisible Lord himself. We are aware of the relevance of his activity and his promises for ourselves and for the world in general (Heb 11.1).

So the people who were told, 'Your faith has made you well' must have been those who, having stopped looking to their own resources, were focusing in total trust on Jesus and abandoning themselves to God's grace.

Whose faith?

Who needs to exercise faith for healing? In the Bible healing takes place in the context of people looking in full trust to God. In Scripture this attitude is expressed by the one seeking healing, or by a group of people, or by the one who is praying for the sick person.

One example of someone exercising faith on behalf of someone else was the centurion who asked Jesus for help. The incident shows that although the laying-on of hands is very valuable as an aid to faith, it is possible for someone to be healed at a distance. People don't have to be fit enough to endure a 'healing meeting' before they can be cured!

The centurion had a paralysed servant back home who was in terrible suffering. So eager was Jesus to heal that he did not wait to be asked. It was sufficient that this man had placed the need of an individual before him. Jesus said he would go and heal the man. Exercising great faith in Jesus, and perhaps also respect for current Jewish beliefs about ceremonial uncleanness, the centurion told Jesus that it wouldn't be necessary for him to enter his Gentile house: he would only have to say the word of healing from a distance. Would *we* have reacted like that, or would we have replied to Jesus, 'that's just what my servant needs; he needs you to come and physically touch him'? When the centurion sent orders to soldiers under his command, they would jump to attention and obey immediately. By faith he knew that Jesus had authority over life and health; he too could send orders which would be obeyed immediately. After the centurion had said this, Jesus said to him, '"Go! It will be done just as you believed it would." And his servant was healed at that very hour' (Mt 8.13).

In this example a single individual exercised faith on behalf of someone who wasn't present. There is no need to believe that Jesus can only heal those who are physically near to us.

When Peter and John were going to the Temple to pray, they said to a lame beggar who had shown no faith but had only asked for money: 'In the name of Jesus Christ of Nazareth, walk' (Acts 3.6). Peter seems to be the only person here who exercised faith, but the lame man immediately got up and walked. That the man gained faith is implied by his reaction of praising God (v8) and by continuing to be associated with believers (Acts 4.14). So we see that an unbeliever can be healed, and even brought to faith through his own healing.

Sometimes an isolated individual can be the one showing the necessary faith for healing without any encouragement from other believers. In the Gospels we read of an individual who was isolated from society because of her complaint. She broke all the social taboos and pushed through a crowd and touched Jesus.

She was expressing faith in Jesus for *herself*. By faith she knew that if she but touched his clothes she would be healed. Jesus felt that power had gone out of him. He made the woman identify herself, for her own good. She was in a ceremonially unclean condition and she knew that she shouldn't even have been in the crowd, let alone touching and therefore defiling a 'holy man'. If she had crept off, she would have had a healed body but also a troubled conscience for the rest of her life. So Jesus brought her out into the open so that she would know that he was aware of exactly what had happened and thoroughly approved of her action. He said to her, 'Daughter, your faith has healed you. Go in peace, and be freed from your suffering' (Mk 5.21–34); and she went away with her head held high.

Jesus looked for faith being exercised. When men lowered the paralysed man through the flat roof where he was teaching, Jesus noticed their faith (Mk 2.5). When Paul was at Lystra he could tell that the lame man there had faith and so he pronounced healing (Acts 14.8–10).

Gill's story
Sometimes the person can have an unformed expectation of what is going to happen, but nevertheless have the assurance that the best thing to do is to look in faith to Jesus. My wife, Irene, and I once prayed for a woman in our front room. Gill had had polio and her leg was in a calliper. Her legs were of unequal length, so one shoe was built up approximately an inch so that she could walk better. She did not feel very well, so we prayed for her. There was a wonderful peace as we prayed. She felt better and thought that possibly her leg had lengthened

a minute amount but wasn't sure. The next day her leg was causing her real discomfort so she went to her doctor in the hospital. He took her calliper off and scientifically measured her leg. The cause of her discomfort was that her shorter leg had grown about an inch and the calliper needed to be re-adjusted! She wrote to me, so I will let her tell her tale in her own words.

Over the years I had much prayer for healing, some of which has produced obvious results immediately, and some not till later, or not at all yet.

In June 1983 I went to see Donald partly for prayer for physical healing but also because I was feeling quite down. For various reasons I was feeling rejected and hurt and felt I needed prayer for this.

As we started praying God encouraged through words that Donald and Irene gave me, saying that, although I felt hurt and rejected, God was going to use it for his glory. God also told me that his name for me was 'Not Forgotten'. At this point I 'zonked out', or to be more technical started to rest in the Spirit. I wasn't aware of what was going on around me but I had the most wonderful feeling of being loved. When I came out of this rest Donald and Irene said that they had prayed for my leg to grow – the left leg was one inch shorter than the other. I don't think my response was particularly full of faith but I waited to see what would happen. Within a few days, I had backache (a not unusual occurrence) and went to see my GP (a Christian). I said that my leg had been prayed for, for lengthening, so he measured my legs and discovered that they were both the same length, and this was confirmed a month later by my specialist at the hospital.

This incident occurred shortly before I was to be married, and God gave me an additional wedding present because of it. As my left leg had grown, I no longer needed a built-up boot on it, so I had to have new ones made and the hospital agreed that I could have them made in white leather to match my wedding dress. What a blessing!

Often, when we are wanting healing, it is sufficient just to ask the Lord to be present in his loving power. It was enough for those four men to lower the paralysed man through the roof and land him at Jesus' feet. Jesus took the hint!

Sometimes we are not given any insight into what God is going to do: he does not lead us into any specific petition. Our faith is then expressed by looking confidently to Jesus to do the best for the person concerned.

Alan, a middle-aged man came, with his wife, to our front-room. He was really broken-hearted, having suffered the recurrence of various types of cancer and gone frequently into hospital for treatment. He was convinced that, as a result of his enforced absence, he would lose his job in a merger. He had just received more medical evidence of another malignant cancer of a different type. His whole body seemed to have no resistance whatever to the disease.

We prayed concerning his ability to trust the Lord for the future and for him to receive God's peace immediately. In a matter of minutes, his whole demeanour had changed. None of us was sure what the Lord was going to do for him, but it was clear that the peace of God was reigning in his heart.

He fulfilled his next hospital appointment only to be told that the cancer had disappeared. We asked ourselves, 'Is this just temporary remission?', but rather than guess, we continued to praise God for what he was doing in Alan's body.

Alan's story

I saw him four years later: he had no cancer and was a
very active preacher. Here is his own account of what
happened:

> In the days just before Christmas 1967, after the symp-
> toms had become more and more desperate and urgent,
> the urological consultant made the diagnosis of cancer in
> the urinary tract. The biopsy showed it was a virulent
> form of growth which 'seeded' into more growths very
> rapidly. He skilfully 'picked them off' by diathermy only
> to find a week later that there were as many again to treat
> and so it was obvious to him that a course of radiotherapy
> was indicated. The prescription was for a hundred min-
> utes of exposure to cobalt-60 over a period of five weeks at
> Cookridge Regional Hospital in Leeds. That completed, I
> was back at work very quickly and I tried to forget about
> it: 'Just one of those things,' I thought, 'And over now.'
>
> Although all seemed well and I was on an increasingly
> extended regime of examinations under general anaes-
> thetic, I was never able to go for twelve months at a stretch
> without symptoms recurring. After six, maybe seven,
> months, there would be pain, but more frightening,
> haemorrhaging and this would set the train of worry up all
> over again; not just for me – the worry was even greater, I
> know, for Margaret (my wife) and our two teenage daugh-
> ters. Throughout the long years, my family never com-
> plained about having to watch it all happening, feeling
> unable to do very much except hope that all would be well.
> I was thirty-nine years old when it all began.
>
> After what we had expected to be just another cysto-
> scopic examination and treatment to suppress the symp-
> toms, the consultant broke the news: 'We need to operate.
> The right kidney is in trouble.' The next few days were
> taken up with having renal arteriograms and other tests
> which confirmed that surgery was a matter of urgency.

Within a fortnight I had 'lost' the cancerous kidney and was feeling awkward with a 'knit one, pearl one; repeat twenty-six times!' holding the abdominal incision together, extending halfway around my body. I felt physically violated, but the seriousness of that operation did not fully dawn on me. It had not escaped Margaret, though, or the girls. 'Oh well, that's over,' I thought and went back to work as quickly as I could. That was in 1980.

In 1982 yet another primary tumor was found. This was treated successfully with mild chemotherapy. But in 1983 yet another, a fourth primary of yet different genus, was discovered. I began to realise then that cancer had been a key element for fifteen years and would continue to be for the rest of my life, be it long or short.

We went to a healing service at the church we attended most Sunday evenings and there received laying on of hands and anointing by Bishop Morris Maddocks. The service was also to pray for the healing of David Watson, whose dire illness had just been made public.

Then two months brought another trip to the operating theatre with no improvement. Another two months and there was still no change.

Margaret had got to know Donald Werner through an autumn course he had run on the gifts of the Spirit and she suggested I go to see Donald myself, which I was somewhat reluctant to do. After all, I was under the care of a first-class consultant who was carefully monitoring what was happening, so what more could be done? Donald invited us to meet him and his wife Irene for an evening to share our problem and to pray together about it.

The evening was peaceful and relaxing and we talked about the situation – and my job, which was becoming increasingly demanding with the reorganisation of secondary education. After seventeen years as head and knowing of at least one school that was to close through reorganisation, and with the authorities fully aware of the condition of my health – what was the point of my even participating in the imminent reorganisation with any enthusiasm at all?

There was a lot to think about and I don't think I was particularly good company for anyone, having become almost constantly deeply depressed and beginning to lack any hope for the immediate future, let alone the longer-term outlook. At fifty-five I had nothing much to look forward to. My wife and my family, yes, they were (and are) vitally important, but I was sure my days were limited and I hadn't the strength to fight anything any more. But it was good to be able to share all these thoughts and fears with Donald, and with Irene and Margaret (our daughters were both married by now and living quite a distance away).

We prayed and I felt a deep peace at the end of the evening. Looking back, that was the turning point for my health, though I was not aware of it at the time. At the time it just seemed like an evening of peace with the reduction of fear.

I was due for another cystoscopy to see how things were faring and I went into the theatre with no expectation of good news. But when the consultant saw me back on the ward afterwards he said, 'It isn't there any more. You're clear. See you in two months!' He was a man of few words but those words came as a relief. I had already told the LEA that I wished to relinquish my job and so remove a major source of worry.

I find the whole question of healing a mystery. Although I had the best medical treatment and supervision possible, that in itself didn't produce a deep-down 'cure'. Was it a combination of excellent medical care, release from some enormous pressures of work and the faith of others in the healing power of God? And, I guess, it's still a mystery to me; a mystery, yet somehow the cycle of events seems so obvious, almost rational, now.

But here we are 1988, coming up to my fifty-fourth

general anaesthetic and still no recurrence and I'm symptom-free. I'm on a one-year regime for check-ups and I'm well into the fifth year of full remission. It is truly beyond my understanding why David Watson was not healed and I was.

One discovery I have made is that God's world doesn't fall into the patterns of rational human understanding. The kingdom of God is not a democracy: it's a benevolent dictatorship and all we can do is to keep trying our utmost to go his way. I have failed badly in this, I know, and I guess I will go on failing. Perhaps that's what having human nature involves. But I'm now more conscious of the ways in which I fail and so consciously seek to know what he wants of me, together with his power to do his will.

Alan's experience highlights the importance of not confusing what our imagination tells us with what the Lord says. We must live and pray in the real world. If the Lord wants to speak to us, or give us a word of knowledge as we pray, he will, in one way or another. However if he does not speak, we can wait patiently until what he is doing becomes obvious! We should listen to the Lord and not our imaginations; neither should we become the victims of auto-suggestion. We are called to have faith in a person and not in a process.

Negative influences and attitudes
If faith in Jesus is important for healing, then the lack of faith is not just neutral: it actually hinders healing. Not to trust in Christ brings harm to people.

When we pray for people, it is helpful to ask any hardened unbelievers who are present to leave while we pray. There is a good precedent for this. Jesus went to bring Jairus' daughter back to life. When he expressed his faith that she would soon be wide awake and healthy again, he was met with sceptical laughter. He then told everyone to leave except Peter, James and John and the girl's parents. They alone were to remain with him as he prayed for Jairus' daughter and woke her out of death (Mk 5.35–43).

Harmful opposition was also experienced by Jesus when he ministered in his home town of Nazareth. People acknowledged his wisdom and miraculous powers, but they failed to put their faith in him as a person. They were limited in their vision by their human knowledge of his boyhood and his family, and were offended when they thought that he was acting in a way that was inconsistent with his humble background. They could not honour him as a prophet. In their eyes he was not a special messenger from God. As they were unable to recognise his authority they had no faith in him. The result of this was that even Jesus could not do many miracles among them. The negative effect of hostile unbelief restricted his healing ministry (Mt 13.53–58).

There is no evidence that Jesus was ever angry because *sick* people showed a lack of faith. He was even firmly reassuring to the man who was in two minds about whether Jesus could heal his boy or not. The man said, 'I do believe; help me overcome my unbelief!' (Mk 9.24). He had just been with Jesus' disciples, who had proved powerless to do anything to help. Jesus, furious at the unbelief of his *disciples*, which had meant that the boy had not been cured, said 'O unbelieving generation . . . how long shall I stay with you? How long shall I put up with you?' (Mk 9.19). They had to learn what prayer was all about, as Jesus told them later.

It is important to have faith in Jesus himself and not

to place our faith in a healing technique to be applied in all situations. It is dangerous to repeat other people's catch-phrases as if they had some intrinsic power or would be far better than our own words and phrases. It is easy to think that if we copy what someone else has done 'successfully', we will have the same results. But this isn't necessarily the case. The all-important element is not the *method* used but the faith exercised.

It is possible to pray without this faith and call out 'in the name of Jesus' as if using some talisman. This was the approach of the seven sons of Sceva when attempting exorcisms. They would say, 'In the name of Jesus, whom Paul preaches, I command you to come out' (Acts 19.13). But the demons, rather than obeying the command, attacked the people using the name. Ephesus was full of people practising magic, but Christians today can also use the name of Jesus as though it were a magic spell. Rather, when we use Jesus' name, we should be 'saying' that we have faith in his character and authority. If we lack such faith we should not use the name.

The early disciples sometimes showed great faith in Jesus by using his name when they pronounced healing. Peter, for example, explained how a man had been healed: 'By faith in the name of Jesus, this man whom you see and know was made strong. It is Jesus' name and the faith that comes through him that has given this complete healing to him, as you can all see' (Acts 3.16).

Jesus never refused to pray for those who came to him for healing. He never rebuked them for lack of faith. We would do well to follow his example. Normally it is sufficient in itself if people come and ask us as Christians to pray for them. They are looking, however hesitatingly, to Jesus for healing. They are asking us to contact him with them. If absence of faith is the reason for a person's lack of healing, it could be the 'fault' of the person who is ministering rather than of the sick person. It is cowardly, as well as being in error, to place blame on the sick people. It is wrong to let them go away, not only with the original sickness, but also with a sense of guilt or inferiority about their so-called lack of faith.

What price medicine?

Does it show a lack of faith to use medical treatment? The short answer is that it can but needn't. In the Old Testament, we have the case of Asa with his foot trouble. We find that he was condemned, not for turning to the physicians for help, but because he didn't turn to the Lord. 'Though his disease was severe, even in his illness he did not seek help from the Lord, but only from the physicians' (2 Chr 16.12). Our trust should always be placed in the Lord, who is the source of all health and healing. We may value the physician as someone used by the Lord to bring about our healing, but he must never be regarded as an alternative way of obtaining healing if God will not heal us. There are some good words in the Apocrypha about treating a physician with the highest esteem as an agent of the Lord, especially if he is also a man of prayer (Ecclesiasticus 38.1–14).

King Hezekiah prayed to the Lord for healing. The Lord promised to heal him of what otherwise would have been a fatal illness and gave him another fifteen years to live. Hezekiah was given a sign that he would be healed. It was in the form of a moving shadow.

Nevertheless the prophet Isaiah also acted like a physician and made a poultice of figs and applied it to Hezekiah's boil and he recovered. Here we find a uniting of prayer, signs and wonders and medicine as an expression of faith in the Lord (2 Kg 20.1–11).

The apostle Paul gave 'medical advice' to Timothy about his stomach and his frequent illnesses (1 Tim 5.23) in a letter in which he encouraged him to be strong in faith (1 Tim 6.11). Clearly Paul saw nothing wrong or substandard in taking medicine that had been produced from materials originally created by God. In fact Paul had a very positive attitude – one of real affection – to a particular physician, his fellow-labourer whom he calls 'our dear friend Luke, the doctor' (Col 4.14). The implication was that he was a practising doctor.

Jim Glennon, in guidelines for those who are receiving medical treatment and who wish to draw on the healing ministry, writes:

> Continue to draw on the medical treatment as prescribed by the doctor and do it with a good conscience.
>
> Tell the doctor that you are attending a service of divine healing and keep him informed as to the results.
>
> Do not let the medical prognosis limit your faith expectation.
>
> Look past the treatment and prognosis to God and believe that, with him, all things are possible. Let that become the measure and reality of your faith (*Your Healing is Within You*, p 131).

We should have faith in the person of Jesus, and this means that we should be glad to receive healing from him by whatever means he should choose. Sometimes he heals in answer to words of prayer alone and at other times in answer to prayer and actions such as laying on of hands or anointing with oil. Sometimes he works through the 'natural' means and healing agents he has built into the created order and/or through medicine and doctors. Whatever the means, we place our faith in him alone: 'I am the Lord who heals you' (Ex 15.26).

Faith and obedience

Faith and obedience are inextricably linked. Obedience is saying to the Lord in our actions that we have faith in him; that we believe he would only tell us to do the best thing in any situation and would not tell us to do what we would find impossible or harmful. When we know what the Lord is saying to us, it should create in us sufficient faith to obey him.

One Sabbath Jesus went to the synagogue where a trap had been set for him by the religious leaders (Lk 6.6–11). They had been misusing the Sabbath to plan how to trick Jesus. A man, sitting in the synagogue, had a shrivelled hand. The religious leaders may even have carefully placed the man so that Jesus would have been bound to notice him. They were preoccupied with finding something of which they could accuse Jesus when they should have been devoted to worshipping the Lord on the day of rest. They wondered whether Jesus would do the work of a healer on the Sabbath. If he laid hands on the man, they could accuse him of working.

Jesus took the opportunity to point out that failing to take an opportunity to do good is in fact doing evil; failing to save life is in fact destroying it. Which was the better way to keep the Sabbath? Was it by doing good and saving life, or by doing evil and destroying life? Jesus asked these questions. Then, fully aware of the hostile company, he simply said to the man, 'Stretch out your hand'. Nobody would be able to call *that* work!

The man did as he was told. In his resolve to obey Jesus he was expressing faith in him. The religious leaders who were disobedient to God were furious, but the man who obeyed Jesus was healed.

We all need to come to Jesus believing that he will heal us and those for whom we pray. Faithlessness does harm to our health and wellbeing. When we know what the Lord wants us to do, our faith is not to be expressed just in words but in obedient actions. Then we can make the psalmist's song our own: 'I will exalt you, O Lord, for you lifted me out of the depths and did not let my enemies gloat over me. O Lord my God, I called to you for help and you healed me' (Ps 30.1–2).

Chapter 13

A HAUNTED HEART

'Of course there are *white* witches,' said a nursery-school teacher to our four-year-old daughter. Her attempt at indoctrination was well meant. She wanted our daughter to be able to distinguish between evil and good witches, so that she would turn to the right type in the day of need.

In the London parish in which I minister, it is a socially accepted practice to join a large gathering on Saturday nights and listen to what messages a medium might receive 'from the beyond'. The human circumstances that have led to this popular activity are easy to understand. Some dear relation dies and their loved ones are cut off from that person for ever. They may not have received any clear teaching from the church about the after-life or they may not believe such teaching. Either way, they are offered the joyful possibility of making contact with the departed. Many find this really comforting. They hear the familiar voice again, telling them things that only he or she could know.

Sandra's story

This was the experience of someone I now know well.

We will call her Sandra. She writes her own account of what happened.

I turned to spiritualism after the death of my parents and became involved in this area of the occult for almost eleven years. I had been guided to spiritualism by well-meaning friends, who marvelled at the comfort it was able to offer to people who had been recently bereaved. I attended a seance and was amazed at the accuracy of the messages I was given. In order to learn more about 'life on the other side', I attended many meetings and seances and read all the literature that I could find. I received enough convincing answers to furnish me with the 'proof' for which I was seeking, and from this I obtained the comfort and reassurance that I so desperately needed. My grief was eased and I was happy to be told that my parents were still very much with me, albeit unseen: I was also told that it cost them a great deal of effort to communicate and for this reason it was important that I should remain open and receptive to them. To have turned my back on spiritualism at this stage would have seemed like an act of betrayal to my parents and I was torn between my love for them and the fear that spiritualism brought to me. Amazingly, I never once questioned why something that could give such comfort should prove to be so fearful. The fear also acted as a magnet to other areas of the occult and I became attracted to clairvoyance, tarot cards and astrology.

My first steps towards Christianity came about by a chance meeting with an acquaintance and an invitation to attend a guest service at St George the Martyr Church in Queen Square. I didn't really want to go but lacked a good excuse to get out of it. I couldn't believe how marvellous the service was and how much I enjoyed it and I walked home afterwards feeling uplifted and totally calm. It was also very apparent from my first visit to church that the

God who sent his only son, Jesus Christ, to be sacrificed for the sin of the world, was not the same god that I had been taught about through spiritualism. I wanted to know more about Jesus Christ and became a regular attender at church. I began to study the Bible at home and realised that the whole area of my life connected with spiritualism was under satanic influence, but that Christ was able to redeem me from all this through his love and forgiveness, which knows no bounds. I accepted Christ into my life and was reborn into the Christian faith. I knew that my past involvement with the occult had been a great sin, and I trusted Jesus to carry me forward in faith without fear of condemnation.

During the first few months of my new life in the Christian faith, I experienced the total peace that only Christ's love for us can bring, and I was helped and encouraged very much by fellow-Christians within the church body. However, it was as I began to grow in faith that I noticed that troubles appeared to be directing themselves at me. For every step taken forward in faith, I seemed to be knocked back three by trouble. I started having difficulty in studying the Bible and was often hit by blinding headaches the minute I opened it. My concentration during the sermons at church was ruined by tickling coughs in my throat or pains in my back. A friend lent me some tapes on the healing ministry of Jesus but the batteries often ran out in my cassette player; on one occasion the whole tape came spilling out. The more I asked for help with these troubles, the harder the troubles hit me and for this reason I eventually stopped asking people to pray for me. Fear hit me once again and I tried to be a very quiet Christian without attracting too much attention to myself, but troubles arrived from every direction.

My family began to be affected by various worries and troubles and I carried the guilt of thinking that this was all happening because of me. I suffered long bouts of insomnia, alternating with nightmares featuring my mother accusing me of abandoning and betraying her. I was in a state of limbo – unable to go back to my old way of life, because I now knew the truth, but unable to go any further forward in faith, because fear prevented me from doing so. I began to wonder why Christ was allowing this to happen to me and decided that I probably just wasn't good enough to become a Christian and seriously questioned the depth of my faith. Eventually, I found the courage to speak to Donald Werner about my confusion and he invited me to his house so that I could talk further with him and his wife, Irene.

I went to his house in the hope that he wouldn't pray for me. I didn't mind speaking about things, but really didn't want to invite any more trouble by praying about them. Donald and Irene listened patiently while I went through the whole episode of my fear and troubles. They spoke at great length of the love of Jesus Christ and his victory on the cross over sin; and how Christians are able to go boldly forward in faith without fear or guilt because Christ had already dealt with this. He then asked me if I had really given up the whole area of my involvement with spiritualism to God and asked for his forgiveness on this. I answered 'no' to both questions. Even though I knew that my involvement had been a very great sin, I was unable to repent because it had, at the time, brought me comfort and to repent of that would seem like a betrayal to my parents. For the same reason, I was unable to ask God's forgiveness for something that I was unable to be sorry for, even though I knew it was a sin, and I hoped that God would accept me just as I was. Almost as soon as I had said the words, I realised that this was the area in which Satan still had me bound, and that he was using the love that I had for my parents to trap me in the fear of letting go. When Mr Werner said almost exactly the same words to me, it was as though I was hearing them for the second time.

We began to pray and it was at this point that I began to feel slightly afraid and trapped. To make things easier for me, Mr Werner suggested that I repeat the words after him, renouncing the devil and all his works, repenting of my involvement in this area and handing the whole thing over to God to receive his forgiveness. Panic really hit me and lengthy silences followed as I struggled to get the words out that stuck in my throat. I knew that it was really important that I should trust in God during this time of prayer in order that I could be set free. Suddenly the words that came from my lips had meaning in my heart and I could feel the fear being swallowed up by total calm and peace. By the time we had finished praying, this whole area of my life had been handed over to the Lord, the burden had been taken off me and I had asked for, and received, God's loving forgiveness. Through Jesus Christ I had finally been set free and guilt and fear no longer had any hold over me.

Over a year has passed since then and I am very happy to say that I am still growing in faith, still wondering at God's marvellous and mighty works and still putting my trust firmly in him. He hasn't kept a record of all my wrongdoings but has wiped the slate clean, and in him I am a new creation. I praise God for his love for me and gladly and freely follow him in the sure knowledge that he will never betray my trust and that his love is everlasting.

The Bible and mediums

Sandra was delivered from the hostile spirit-world. The Bible says that these 'familiar' spirits really exist. It teaches that they impart knowledge supernaturally to the medium and often mimic the voice of the departed to such an extent that people falsely believe there is actual contact with the departed person.

It is partly because the whole process of mediumistic consultation with the departed is based on an unrecognised deception that it is condemned by the Lord. 'Let no-one be found among you who . . . is a medium or spiritualist or who consults the dead. Anyone who does these things is detestable to the Lord' (Deut 18.10–12). 'Do not turn to mediums or seek out spiritualists, for you will be defiled by them' (Lev 19.31). 'I will set my face against the person who turns to mediums and spiritualists to prostitute himself by following them, and I will cut him off from his people' (Lev 20.6).

This condemnation of mediumistic practices is not just confined to the early books of the Bible: it is found throughout. Isaiah the prophet condemns it and tells us where we should positively seek guidance and, also, what is the destiny of such mediums: 'When men tell you to consult mediums and spiritualists, who whisper and mutter, should not a people enquire of their God? Why consult the dead on behalf of the living? To the law and the testimony! If they do not speak according to this word, they have no light of dawn . . . they will be thrust into utter darkness' (Is 8.19–22).

This advice is ignored by many today, who persist in acting as King Saul did. 'Saul died because he was unfaithful to the Lord; he did not keep the word of the Lord, and even consulted a medium for guidance, and did not enquire of the Lord' (1 Chr 10.13).

Many mediums are so misguided as to imagine that their spiritualist practices are a means of seeking the mind of the Lord. Instead of seeing mediumistic activity as anathema to God, they even begin some of their public meetings with prayer to God! Could there be a state of greater deception than that? Notice that in the Bible the mediums are not necessarily condemned for immorality, or for wanting to do people any harm, but are condemned for just practising their mediumistic arts. Such practices in themselves are seen to be evil and contrary to God's word. The only godly answer for someone who has such a familiar spirit is to seek deliverance from it. To such a spirit the apostle Paul said: ' "In the name of Jesus Christ, I command you to come out of her!" At that moment the spirit left her' (Acts 16.18).

There is much confused thinking in this area. In the official biography of Harry Edwards, the famous English mediumistic healer, published by the Spiritualist Press, we read the statement: 'In my view this is the same divine power which streamed through the healer of Nazareth in Bible days and produced results that the orthodox regard as miracles.' The writer of those words failed to realise that people 'healed' through mediumistic forces suffer an utter collapse of real faith in Christ as Lord and Saviour. The biographer unwittingly gives the reason for this when he says that spiritual healing is dependent in no way at all on 'the Christian theory of vicarious atonement, under which Jesus was supposed to take all the sins of mankind on his shoulders'. This could not differ more from the Christian belief that sickness is a result of individual and/or corporate sin, and that the atonement won by Jesus on the cross is the means through which all true healing flows.

As explained in detail in chapters two and three, healing in its fullness cannot be experienced until there is a healing of the broken-off relationship between man and God and this can only occur through the only mediator between man and God, the only one who can restore that relationship, namely Jesus Christ who died for us (Gal 3.1, 20; 1 Tim 2.5; Heb 8.6; 9.15).

We are warned by Jesus that 'false Christs and false prophets will appear and perform great signs and miracles to deceive even the elect – if that were possible' (Mt 24.24).

Distinguishing false from true healings

How can we know whether a healing is from God or not? The key is in the biography of Harry Edwards. The false teachers are those who deny that we have been 'bought' with the blood of Jesus (2 Pet 2.1–3), or that Jesus is God incarnate (1 Jn 4.2, 3; Jn 1.1, 14).

The way to discern whether the healer is using mediumistic means of 'healing' or if he is a true servant of Jesus Christ is not merely by the manifestations that take place. Nearly all the manifestations that take place in charismatic healing meetings can be closely paralleled with what happens in mediumistic healings. This can be very disconcerting at times. The devil is called the 'father of lies' and of deception. When some religious leaders thought that God was their father, Jesus told them that it was not God but the devil who was their father. If God has been their Father then they would have been able to hear what Jesus was saying about himself. Everyone who belongs to God believes Jesus and so listens to God speaking through him (Jn 8.42–47). The devil subtly disguises himself in order that he might even deceive people into thinking that he

is an angel of light (2 Cor 11.14). He has even instigated
a counterfeit 'signs and wonders' ministry of his own
(Mt 24.24; Mk 13.33; 2 Thess 2.9; Rev 13.10; 16.14).

Anyone trying to perpetuate a fraud will make the
counterfeit almost identical to the original. Someone
might try to forge a £10 note but would not try to make
an £11 note! The devil is too subtle to make his decep-
tions obvious. For every gift of the Spirit there is a close
counterfeit. Take the marvellous God-given gift of
tongues. Its counterfeit can keep people away from
Jesus and the assurance of salvation. Then there is the
word of knowledge. When the Spirit gives a Christian
such a word, he may see it written above the head of a
person whom it concerns; the same manifestations can
appear to mediums. Again, often the Spirit comes upon
people giving them a great sensation of warmth; and
when an individual has the full attention of the medium, there can be warmth too. Also, the Spirit gives
insight to those seeking to help someone; and a
medium, through a familiar spirit, often knows secret
information about an individual.

What is the best course then? Should we play safe
and avoid using the gifts of the Spirit for fear of the
counterfeit gifts? No; we should earnestly desire spiritual gifts (1 Cor 14.1) and not be robbed, out of fear of
the devil's activity of the wonderful 'tools' God has
given us to express his love. If we based our lives on
such fear we would hold back from committing
ourselves to the gospel of truth, from receiving forgiveness of sins and from giving ourselves to God for his use
(Acts 26.18).

Our lives shouldn't be controlled by fear of the devil
and his counterfeit activities. The Lord encouraged us

to assess the value of a ministry by its results (Mt
7.15–20). There are certain questions we should ask.
Does the use of the gift of tongues bring the person into
a close personal prayer-relationship with Jesus? Does
the healing or the word bring the person to experience
the love of God more? Are there any conversions result-
ing from the healings? Although not everyone whom
Christ healed followed him, some did. So if nobody is
converted to Christ as the result of a healing ministry, it
must be very suspect.

We must not be glib about the subtlety of the devil.
He will deliberately seek to possess people. If he is
dispossessed of his home in a person when they become
a Christian, he will still seek to oppress that person. We
are called to resist this formidable and noisy enemy of
ours. We are to exercise faith (1 Pet 5.8).

Mental illness or demons?

This raises the whole question of how we know whether
a person is demonised, oppressed by the devil or suffering from extreme mental or emotional disorder. This is
not easy, because, as we have seen, the physical, mental, emotional and spiritual aspects of a person interact
with one another. If one aspect is affected, there will be
repercussions in the others. If someone is demonised,
for example, he will also be emotionally disturbed and
this will affect him physically too.

Usually if someone claims to be possessed, he nearly
always isn't! The person concerned does not usually
know that he is possessed and certainly would not
broadcast the fact. When I was in York, someone came
into my office wanting help. He didn't claim to be
possessed but he clearly was. He was into automatic

handwriting and having the most horrific dreams at night. I commanded the evil spirits to leave in the name of Jesus, and after a certain amount of snorting they left. I then prayed for him to be cleansed by the blood of Jesus. The man became a Christian and gave his whole life over to the Lord. As we continued to pray, the Lord told me that the task was not yet finished, and he highlighted the passage of scripture when the evil spirits were cast out of a house, which was then cleaned but left empty for even more spirits to enter (Mt 12.43–45). It was not enough to bind the devil and plunder his goods (Mt 23.22–28). People need more than deliverance and cleansing; they need filling. I prayed for the man to be filled with the Holy Spirit. This occurred instantly and he spoke in other tongues to the glory of God. He had such joy in prayer that it overflowed in praise to God.

How could I be sure that this man was not just mentally and emotionally disturbed? All too often people are described as possessed or demonised or oppressed, when they are not. Some guidelines might be helpful, but it is all-important in any situation to keep praying for the Lord to give us discernment.

When we pray for someone who is oppressed by demons, there is usually great opposition. If, however, the person is suffering from a mental illness then he or she usually calms down when prayer is made. The demonised person will act in a hostile way but, after the time of prayer is over, be unaware of what was done, or realise but apologise, saying it was unintentional – something made them do it.

Someone who was oppressed by evil spirits had arranged to come to my home where my wife and I were to pray for her. She was very apprehensive because she did not know what was wrong with her. To frighten her off, the devil gave her a dream of Irene and me praying dramatically for her deliverance. When she came to our home, we did pray for her deliverance but in a completely undramatic way and a deep peace descended upon her. Now, six years later, she is still walking in the liberty the Lord gives her.

Another indication of demonic activity is when the person prayed for falls into a trance: a counterfeit of resting in the Spirit. When resting in the Spirit, people can hear what is being said to them, know the presence of Jesus and listen and respond to the Word of God being spoken. At such times promises from Scripture have a powerful effect on the individual. In a demon-induced trance, the person is deaf to God's Word and to prayer; he may appear to be totally unconscious. Sometimes when the name of Jesus is being used in prayer another voice speaks from within the person being prayed for, saying that he or she cannot stand the name. People who are mentally ill do not react in these ways.

Note too that these manifestations only occur if the person praying is a genuine Christian. If he is an unbeliever or only a nominal Christian who does not know the indwelling power of the Holy Spirit, the demon is totally unthreatened and does not react from within the person. The spirits concerned may feel more powerful than those who are trying to expel them. If that is the case they may take the offensive, as the sons of Sceva found out to their cost (Acts 19.13–16).

We should be sure that God is calling us to this work

before we get involved. We must know that we can exercise complete faith in God in this area and that we are not trying to escape into the realm of the spectacular because our Christian walk is not sufficiently exciting. We must beware of doing uncommissioned work of any sort, including this.

The characteristic behaviour of someone who is demonised is very clearly shown, for example, by the Gerasene man who met Jesus (Mk 5.1–12). He is described as demon-possessed (v16). There are eight points worth noticing.

We are told that the man had an unclean spirit: this means that inside him was another being (v2).

He had supernatural physical strength beyond that of a normal human being (v3).

He had fits of rage. He could not be subdued and he had the strength to break chains and fetters (v4).

He had a personality at war with itself. He felt compelled to run to Jesus and kneel before him; at the same time, he wanted to be left alone and not tortured by Jesus (vv 6, 7).

He showed hostility towards Jesus (v7).

He had supernatural and accurate knowledge of who Jesus was – 'the Son of the Most High God' (v7).

He probably spoke in a variety of voices because of the multiplicity of demons within him (v9).

There was 'transference' of the demons; they entered a large herd of pigs which were feeding on the nearby hillside (v13).

Mentally disordered people might show some of these characteristics but certainly not the last four.

Power and authority

We should not be marching around like self-appointed spiritual storm-troopers but, if we do come across possessed people, there is no need to be afraid. There is victory and authority in the name of Jesus who, having 'disarmed the powers and authorities . . . made a public spectacle of them, triumphing over them by the cross' (Col 2.15). We can walk with confidence because of that victory and see the application of this victory to bring us to wholeness and freedom. If and when the Lord sends us to pray for the possessed, then he will give the power and the authority which he also gave to the disciples (Lk 9.1–2).

I am reminded of a lorry driver who was handed a letter giving him authority to collect a bull for market. When he got inside the field, the bull decided that the man had no power to collect him. The bull was right. The man had to flee for his life, as he was hotly pursued by the animal. It was no good having authority without the power to enforce it.

Let us make sure that we are commissioned by the Lord before entering this field of delivering people from evil spirits. Let us make sure that we have confidence that Christ has won the victory in this area and that we have the power of God with us. If we are doing the work which the Lord has commissioned us to do, nothing will harm us (Lk 10.19) and we will experience that 'the Lord is faithful, and he will strengthen and protect you from the evil one' (2 Thess 3.3).

In the Lord's service we will know that even principalities and demons cannot separate us from his love. We are secure and safe (Rom 8.37–39); the evil one cannot touch us (1 Jn 5.18, 19). 'The Lord will rescue me from evil attack and will bring me safely to his heavenly kingdom. To him be glory for ever and ever. Amen' (2 Tim 4.18).

Chapter 14

A HEART KEPT HEALTHY

If someone breaks a leg and is put into plaster for a number of weeks, his leg muscles become flabby. When the plaster is removed, exercise is needed before the person is able to walk again properly. The leg may have been set and the bones mended, but more treatment is required.

Every aspect of our beings – spiritual, physical, mental or emotional – needs healthy exercise. When Jesus healed someone, he often told him to start leading a different life. He even told the man at the pool of Bethesda that if he did not stop his habitual sins then he would find himself in a worse state than ever he was before: 'See, you are well again. Stop sinning or something worse may happen to you' (Jn 5.14).

It is clear that Jesus saw healing not as an end in itself. It was a sign of the kingdom of God: a manifestation of God's love and power to restore people. It was also a call to acknowledge the rule of God in people's lives as they enter his kingdom. Healing was seen as the prelude to a person living a new life of obedience to

God. This obedience was to be motivated by love and
gratitude.

Obedience and joy

We are healed in order to obey. Our bodies are healed
in order to obey the Creator's 'blueprint'. Our spirits
are healed so that we can worship and give glory to
God. Our minds and emotions are healed so that we
can think and feel the way God created them to function. Our healing should enable us to walk in agree-
ment with God's desire for us, and to embrace his
intention for our lives. We can only walk with God if we
agree with him. Do two walk together unless they have
agreed to do so (Amos 3.3)? To be a healthy person is to
be like Jesus – someone completely obedient to God,
and whose life says, 'He is Lord'.

Peter's mother-in-law gave a living example of that
truth about healing. She was lying in bed with a fever
and Jesus healed her and immediately she got up and
served him (Mt 8.14).

If we walk close to the Lord we have joy. This joy is
the foretaste of heaven. The Psalmist writes: 'You have
made known to me the path of life; you will fill me with
joy in your presence, with eternal pleasures at your
right hand' (Ps 16.11).

Where there is a sense of emptiness in people it is
usually a sign that they are not walking with the Lord.
Emptiness may have a moral cause.

Jesus met a woman at the well in Samaria and
perceived that she had a desperate inner thirst. He
sensitively steered the conversation to say that he could
give her living water that would satisfy that thirst. First,
she was made to face up to her present situation: she

was trying to get some satisfaction in life by throwing herself at a number of men as temporary 'husbands'. Jesus knew her inside out. Here was someone who was trying to fill an aching void. She was doing it in a sinful way. Jesus knew that she needed to be presented with a better alternative before she would leave her present way of life, even though it was desperately empty.

After her conversation with Jesus, she went to bring others from the nearby village to see him, saying, 'He told me everything I ever did' (Jn 4.39). Jesus had not hesitated to confront her with every detail of her life. The remarkable thing is that he had been able to do so without leaving her feeling hopelessly condemned by him. In fact, she was so thrilled about her conversation with him that she wanted others to find Jesus. They came out of the nearby village to meet him. Their conclusion was that Jesus 'really is the Saviour of the world' (v42c).

Often people feel safe in their immorality because they feel that they can 'get away with it'. However, even if they are not caught out, people who are immoral have a guilty conscience and an emptiness within. We need to realise that nothing is hidden from God, nor shall be hidden (Mt 10.26). The good news, which Jesus brought to people, is that we have the present opportunity to repent and be restored so that we can bring forth the fruits of repentance in an obedient life (Mt 3.8). The presence of Jesus' love and grace encourages us to want to change, just as it encouraged the Samaritan woman to come out of hiding and face the truth so that she could then be set free (Jn 8.32).

In a parable Jesus told, the prodigal son sank very low in the far-off country. In that state, he remembered his father, who – he realised – would probably give him a job as a servant if he went back home. So he returned home, never imagining what an extravagantly loving welcome awaited him.

The father in the parable represents something of God's welcoming of sinners into his kingdom (Lk 15.20). The son was able to enjoy the wholesome dancing of the kingdom instead of the dancing that took place in the distant country.

Healing is something that is very positive. It offers a satisfying alternative way of life. It involves the filling of the person who has been forgiven with the water that satisfies: the filling with the Holy Spirit.

On one occasion Jesus could see hundreds of people going to observe a religious ceremony (Jn 7.37–39). Water, taken from the river Kedron, was poured on the altar and then channelled back to the river. It was an offering of flowing, living water and an acknowledgement that without water there would be no crops or vegetation, and therefore no animals, or human life. The worshippers were expressing their thanks to God for providing them with the needs of life. But there was still within them a great spiritual thirst.

So Jesus stood up and with a loud voice told people to come to him if they were thirsty and he would give them life. In fact the change within them would be so great, he said, that far from being dry their innermost being would become the source of an ever-flowing river. They just had to do two things: first, come to Jesus as thirsty people; second, drink.

Similarly, we can come to the glorified Lord Jesus and 'drink' as he pours the Holy Spirit upon us. The Spirit not only satisfies such drinkers, he also flows out

from them like a stream. There is healing from emptiness and the gift of a new joy as they are filled with the
Holy Spirit (Ac 2.4; 6.5). 'The kingdom of God is . . .
joy in the Holy Spirit' (Rom 14.17). The Lord is ready
to give us the fullness of the Holy Spirit, enabling us to
experience his power within, to be consciously aware of
his indwelling love, and to live the new life of obedience
with joy.

Forgiveness

If there is a blockage to God's Spirit filling us, we need
to find out what it is. The blockage may be that we have
an unforgiving attitude towards somebody. It is important to forgive those who have wronged us. If we do
this, we will be open to experience God's forgiveness; if
we refuse to forgive others, then God will not forgive us
(Mt 6.14, 15).

Jesus told the story of an unforgiving servant who
owed a great debt to his master. When he pleaded for
forgiveness, his master forgave him his debt. The same
man was owed a comparatively trivial amount by a
fellow servant. He would not listen to his fellow servant's pleas, however, and had him imprisoned. Hearing of this, the master was furious and cast into prison
the person whose debts he had forgiven. After telling
this story, Jesus said that our heavenly Father would
treat us like that unless we forgave our brother from our
hearts (Mt 18.35).

Those who refuse to forgive others, become a blockage to the flow of God's forgiveness and remain unforgiven. As we need to be constantly forgiven if we are
to live in the Lord's presence and be filled with his
Spirit, it cannot be overstressed that, for our health

and wellbeing, we need to forgive people – without delay.

Sometimes we may feel emotionally cold towards someone, but the Lord still wants us to set our wills to forgive that person and let God deal with our emotions in his good time. We cannot serve God if we have an unforgiving heart, because this will cut us off from his power. Only through his power, not our own strength, can we serve him. If we harbour a grudge, our souls and bodies will suffer for it; we will lose our joy and become heavy-hearted in our Christian life: 'A cheerful heart is good medicine, but a crushed spirit dries up the bones' (Prov 17.22).

We might say, 'But how long do we have to go on forgiving someone?' The very asking of that question reveals a wrong attitude, as the apostle Peter was to find. If we keep a count of the number of times someone has done something against us, then we are certainly not forgiving and forgetting. Instead we are sort of forgiving and definitely counting! If we forgive some-one, then our attitude to them should be as if they had never done anything that needed forgiveness. After all that is how God treats us in Christ, and he has forgiven us a lot more than we will ever need to forgive others.

The breakdown in relationships is often precipitated by the recurring comment, 'but you always do that – time and time again'. Praise the Lord, he does not treat us like that: there is now no condemnation for those who are in Christ Jesus (Rom 8.1). Much to Peter's surprise he was told not to forgive just seven times but to forgive seventy times seven – *ie*, without number (Mt 18.22). As we forgive others, we will be overwhelmed by the Lord's forgiveness of us and the way he pours his blessings into our lap (Lk 6.37–38). We should be able to pray, 'Father . . . forgive us our trespasses as we (do in practice) forgive those who trespass against us.'

We should forgive others without reluctance. What motivates us to forgive should not be just the threat that if we don't forgive them we will remain unforgiven. Nor should we try to strike a bargain with God as if we are ever in a position to say to God, 'We have forgiven – now it's your turn!' We forgive others because he first forgave us. We are so overwhelmed with gratitude that we feel that the *least* we can do is not to be so small-minded as to bear grudges.

Jesus was once sitting in the house of a Pharisee (Lk 7.36–50) and a woman came and anointed his feet with ointment, tears and kisses. He explained her behaviour: it was, he said, an overflowing of her loving gratitude for having been forgiven of her sins (v17). She would remain forgiven (v48). She would live as a saved and healthy person enjoying the peace of God (v50). She was not only forgiven of her sins. Her tears of love were demonstrating that she was receiving emotional healing.

The Lord wants us to be so full of the Holy Spirit that there is no room for the evil spirits which are able to fill spiritual vacuums (Mt 12.43–45). He does not want to see us trying to compromise, partly living for God and partly open to things that are contrary to his rule in our lives. He does not want his people to become a spreading vine that proudly produces fruit to honour false gods (Hos 10.1, 2). He has planted us to be a vine full of true life and bringing forth the fruit of the Spirit (Gal 5.16–26). The vine's outward appearances can be very misleading. Paul looked deeper to what was below the surface; he warned us about people who hold the form of religion but deny its power. If we are not open to be indwelt by the power of the Spirit, then our lives and attitudes will show that we are really opposed to the truth and have a counterfeit faith. Sooner or later we will be seen for who we are (2 Tim 3.5, 8, 9).

Faith in God

How does being filled with the Holy Spirit enable us to live a healthy life? To be healthy we need to have confidence in what God does and be confident that we are accepted by him. Without the Holy Spirit filling us, we would lack such areas of confidence.

Unless we have faith in God it is impossible to profit from his word and enter into his promises (Heb 4.2). We need to have confidence and trust in him. Of the Lord it is confidently declared: 'You will keep in perfect peace him whose mind is steadfast, because he trusts in you. Trust in the Lord for ever, for the Lord, the Lord, is Rock eternal' (Is 26.3, 4). There has to be faith and trust in any positive relationship.

In marriage both partners might be doing and saying all the right things and be completely loyal to one another. But if one partner loses faith in the other and begins to be suspicious, ceasing to believe the word of the other or explanations given, then the threat of a break-up hangs over that marriage. When we cease to trust God's word, and cannot see that his plan for our life is the best plan possible, then we cannot please him. There must be faith and trust in a healthy relationship.

On the other hand, if there *is* faith, we will have the assurance that we can come to him on the basis of his declared will and receive all the blessing he has promised us (1 Jn 5.14, 15). We know that we are not wasting our time asking for things, in the confidence that he is a Father who loves to give good things to his children (Mt 7.11).

If we have this trust, we can even enjoy things that would otherwise be very threatening. When one of my daughters was just a toddler, I used to throw her high into the air and catch her. I would repeat this 'game' several times. She used to enjoy it so much that she would always shout out, 'More – more'. Her enthusiasm outlasted my energy. She was able to enjoy the experience only because it had never crossed her mind that I would throw her into the air and then walk away. She always landed completely relaxed in my arms. It seems very strange that we react as if our heavenly Father would let us down or betray our trust in him.

Sometimes it is impossible to know *where* the Lord is leading us, but we can still trust him because we know and have experienced that his character is trustworthy. In everyday life we exercise trust on the basis of our experience all the time. For example, in driving along, we might see a hump-backed bridge ahead which obscures our view of the road. But we carry on, confident, on the basis of previous experience, that the road will be there on the other side of the bridge. Similarly, having experienced God's loving hand at work in our lives, we can look forward confidently to the future. Even if we cannot see ahead clearly, God can and he knows best. As Isaac Watts wrote:

> God is our sun and shield,
> Our light and our defence;
> With gifts his hands are filled,
> We draw our blessings thence;

Thrice happy he, O God of hosts,
Whose spirit trusts alone in Thee.

We need to learn to walk by faith and not by sight, until the day when we shall be with the Lord in heaven and see him for ever (2 Cor 5.7).

If we are filled with the Holy Spirit we can not only trust God to guide us but we will also feel 'at home' with him, enjoying the security that results only from a close relationship. Because of his unchanging nature, we know where we stand with him.

The Egyptian gods of Moses' day were held to be very arbitrary in their actions. In one instance, they struck a worshipper blind just for the fun of it! The Lord was very different from these gods. He revealed himself as the 'I AM THAT I AM' – The Eternally Unchanging One – who had a consistent attitude to man. He revealed his nature in the forms of laws, which were not arbitrary statements but expressions of his inner being. He revealed his nature in Jesus Christ who is the same today as he always was; his nature will never change (Heb 13.8), so we know exactly where we stand with him.

If we trust God's unchanging character we can have faith in him during times of perplexity. For example, we may think that we need to understand a situation immediately and so we pray urgently about it. If we do not receive the enlightenment we want there and then, we might well wonder why and whether or not our first prayer was heard.

In Daniel 10.12 the angel from God, while explaining why there had been some delay in his coming to help Daniel, made it clear that from the first day that he had prayed for understanding his words had been heard. Even then, the angel came not too late but at the right time.

We need to ask the Lord to help us to trust his timing. Sometimes we do not even need to know the next step in advance. The Lord will lead us as he sees fit. His enlightenment of our minds never comes too late. In fact, if we are obeying him and if our hearts do not condemn us, we can have every assurance that what we ask in prayer we will receive. When, in the Lord's perfect timing, we *do* receive enlightenment, and as we continue to live in obedience to what he says, our faith will be strengthened by the Holy Spirit (1 Jn 3.21–24).

It often helps us to have assurance that Jesus will heal us if we exercise a 'zoom-lens' faith – one that moves from the general to the particular, and then back to the general. In exercising this kind of faith, we need to affirm our belief that God is the unchanging Lord of all creation and that Jesus Christ is the Saviour of the world; that God is our heavenly Father; that he can heal us; that he can heal a particular part of us. Once we have seen the relevance of his greatness and promises to the particular condition about which we are praying, we can receive all that by faith and start thanking him for his answer in relation to our condition, our lives, other people or the world.

It is difficult to exercise faith for the particular if we don't see it in the context of God Almighty being in control of everything. Faith needs to view a broad canvas, rather than one small detail in the picture. The psalmist used to look at the grandeur of the hills and then realise that the One who had created them – and the whole earth besides – could easily help him (Ps 12.1,

2). It is when we really believe that God works *all* things together for our benefit, that we can be sure of his help when presenting him with a particular need (Rom 8.28).

Because God is unchanging, we can be sure that he will act in the present in a way consistent with what he did in the past. Our past experience of what God has done for us should be recognised as being relevant to our present situation. The greatest thing that God did for us was to give us his Son; so we can be absolutely sure that, having done that for us, he will not withhold any good thing from us (Rom 8.32). Also, the fact that we have experienced God's keeping power, despite all external opposition, will give us the assurance that nothing spiritual or material will be able to separate us from his healing love and power in the future (Rom 8.37–39). Therefore, instead of facing the future with a fear that paralyses us into inaction, we can say with confidence, knowing this to have been our experience in the past: 'I can do everything through him who gives me strength' (Phil 4.13; 2 Tim 4.17, 18).

To summarise – in order for us to be healed of our inner emptiness, which inclined us to sin or brought us under spiritual attack in the past, we must repent, and ask God for healing and for the Holy Spirit to fill us, give us the ability to believe God's Word and be fully assured that he will heal us in his time.

Chapter 15

A CORPORATE HEART

We can never be fully healthy if we remain as isolated individuals, so the Lord has given us the fellowship of his church. The word 'fellowship' is often used in a vague way to represent such activities as having tea or coffee after a church service. The word translated 'fellowship' in our Bibles means 'sharing in the same thing'. It is what Christians have in common that creates fellowship, including especially the fact that they are all 'in Christ' and that they all belong to God Incarnate (1 Jn 1.3, 6, 7). The Word became flesh and dwelt among us (Jn 1.14): he really belonged to our humanity, identifying himself with us throughout his life, as was clearly revealed by his baptism *alongside* sinners and his death on the cross *in the place* of sinners. By expressing solidarity with us, he brought about a new people who have a sense of belonging to him and therefore of belonging to each other.

Much sickness is rooted in people's sense of not belonging, so healing can come when people cease to function as isolated individuals and know that they belong to God. Jesus took our human nature upon himself and redeemed it. He removed our sin so that we could have the experience of belonging to God and to each other. The two are connected: it is impossible to say we love God if we do not love one another (1 Jn 4.7, 8).

The incarnation was man and God in union, not diluting the divinity of God or the humanity of Jesus. Jesus healed not to *prove* who he was but *because* of who he was: the fullness of God, with all his love and grace, walking this earth. He came to restore us to wholeness of being. He was the first of a new humanity – a man united with God. Through him, we can be united with God. Paul describes our lives as being hidden with Christ in God (Col 3.3, 4).

People will come to know God's love as *we* show it to them, in the context of God's people where giving and receiving love is practised. It is not always easy either to show or to receive Christ-like love. Love is costly. It cost Jesus a great deal. Think of how he broke the traditional religious taboos of his day and touched the leper who was regarded as unclean. He chose not to keep to safe superficialities and was prepared to pay the price of expressing a love that could easily be misunderstood or misrepresented. The incarnation was even more costly. It meant getting involved with our messy lives and, ultimately, cost Jesus his life. For Jesus, expressing God's love spelt rejection and crucifixion.

The Christian is called to follow Christ in this type of involvement, both with people inside the church and those outside it. Within the church we need to swallow our pride and be ministered to and minister to others; to wash others' feet and to allow them to wash ours (Jn 13.6–8).

A fellowship of grace

What sort of people do you choose to have fellowship with? To what sort of church do you belong? Do you choose people who think as you do and have the same taste in religious culture as yourself? Or do you see the value of people who are different from yourself?

Jesus chose the company of twelve people who were very different from himself and from each other. They differed in their political opinions and their social standing. Jesus was aware that this was the company that God, his Father, has chosen for him – a fellowship of grace (Lk 6.12–16; Jn 17.6, 12).

Jesus' disciples were a motely crew, judged by human standards. Matthew was a quisling (Lk 5.7–31); Simon, a nationalist, a Zealot (Lk 6.15). The group argued among themselves as to who should be the greatest (Mk 9.33–34). When Jesus told them that he was going to his death in Jerusalem, James and John – to the fury of the others – were concerned only about their future status in the kingdom (Mk 10.35–41).

Then there was Peter, who mistakenly believed he had a superior and unshakeable faith in, and loyalty to, Jesus (Mt 26.33); and Thomas who acknowledged that he found it difficult to believe at all (Jn 20.25). Finally there was Judas, whom Jesus knew, from the beginning, would betray him, but whom he did not eject from the circle of his close friends (Jn 6.64).

Those were Jesus' choice of disciples: the prototype of the Christian church to which we are called to belong. Would your choice have been the same? John Wesley was once asked by a lady if he could direct her to the perfect church. His blunt reply was that if he did know where it was he would not tell her, because she would only spoil it! Too often the church, down the centuries, has been split and split again because of Christians who have been too unloving to live with each other's differences. Even the early church was not without sharp differences at the leadership level; Paul had a head-on collision with Barnabas concerning who was most suitable for a task within the church (Ac 15.39); he also regarded Peter's behaviour as hypocritical at times and told him so publicly (Gal 2.13, 14).

The varied nature of the individuals in the church gives us scope to exercise the grace of forgiveness. We need to let that grace flow freely through us. This involves looking to ourselves. As we minister forgiveness to others, we should also be open to hearing the truth spoken to us and to being changed by it; telling others of their need of healing, should mean being open to healing for ourselves. How can we minister to the speck of sawdust in someone else's eye, if we have a plank sticking out of our own (Mt 7.3–5)? If we avoid forgiving others, then we will be unable to pray the Lord's Prayer and will remain unforgiven by our heavenly Father (Mt 6.12–15).

A fellowship in ministry

Christ has entrusted to the church various gifts and ministries, so that the members may grow up to full maturity (Eph 4.11–13). We may be tempted to think that the gifts we have are not very important and, therefore, never use them. On the other hand, we may feel that we are so gifted that we do not need other people's gifts. Nobody should feel inferior (1 Cor 12.15, 16) and nobody superior (1 Cor 12.21), because we need all the gifts, just as we need each other. We need one another's gift of discernment in deciding what is, or is not, of the Spirit (1 Jn 4.1; Rom 12.2; 1 Thess 5.22). Such 'testing' or assessing is a corporate work of the church, rather than an individual activity.

The Lord has given the church preachers and teachers to turn people's hearts to the truth, to baptise, to teach them that they have been crucified with Christ and raised with him (see chapter 3) and other Christian doctrines. The church also needs those who can counsel, encourage and help people to trust in the Lord to keep them (Ps 55.22); those who will train others in the wearing of their spiritual armour and in the use of the sword of the Spirit (Eph 6.17); those who can lead worship, including particularly the Lord's Supper, at which we remember Jesus in the way he specifically requires of his followers (1 Cor 11.23–25); those who are to be called upon to anoint the sick with oil (Jas 5.14).

For our well-being and that of others, we need to belong to a congregation who are led by people whose ministry we can recognise and derive benefit from, and who recognise and encourage every member's ministry.

A fellowship of love

Jesus taught that the chief commandment was to love God with the whole of our being and each other as ourselves (Mt 22.36–39). He also taught that these two are very similar. We show our love for God by loving each other and, if love is lacking on the human level, then it is also absent in our personal relationship to God.

As the Spirit begins his healing work he heals all the wounds of the past, so removing the causes of our hesitations about loving others. Past hurts make us want to retreat into our shells. But the Spirit pours the healing love of God into our hearts (Rom 5.5) and we are able to risk being vulnerable again.

The heart in the Bible is regarded as the centre of our whole being, not just of our emotions. The prophets spoke of the days in which we live as the time when the Lord would change people's hearts (Eze 11.19) and give them new contrite hearts (Ps 51.17). He is not impressed by any mask we hide behind in pretending to be someone other or different from ourselves; nor is he impressed by outward appearance but looks directly on the heart (1 Sam 16.7). So let's stop trying to hide from him. Instead, let's ask him to search our hearts (Ps 139.23, 24), so that we can be cleansed (Ps 51.10) and have the health and strength we need for walking in the path of God's everlasting love. He can do all that and resolve our inner conflict, so that we are whole within.

This will lead to resolving tensions within the fellowship of God's people. Joining with others who are being healed, we can cast aside our craving for independence and seek the Lord's face together. Then we will experience more of the vastness of the love of God. Paul prayed that this would be the experience of the Ephesian church. 'I pray that you, being rooted and established in love, may have power, together with all the saints, to grasp how wide and long, and high and deep is the love of Christ, and to know his love that surpasses knowledge – that you may be filled in the measure of all the fulness of God' (Eph 3.17–19). When we are 'together with all the saints' we will be overwhelmed by our experience of the depth of God's love for us.

The Lord wants us to be fully healed, so that we can experience and express his love. He has a heart for healing. We have a heart for healing. As we receive healing, we can come together with confidence in prayer, and find all the grace we need (Heb 4.16).

Praise, my soul the King of heaven;
To his feet thy tribute bring.
Ransomed, healed, restored, forgiven,
Who like thee His praise should sing?
Alleluia, Alleluia!
Praise the everlasting King.

CHRISTIAN PRAYER
AND
HEALING

by Andy Arbuthnot

Andy and Audrey Arbuthnot and their team spend many hours each week counselling and praying with those who find their way to the London Healing Mission, which is part of the Church's Ministry of Healing; but this book is not primarily about counselling – it is about praying with power.

A young man said, 'The London Healing Mission is the only place I know where you go in as one person and come out another person.' The reader will find clues as to why in the pages of *Christian Prayer and Healing*.

ISBN 0 946616 59 0

PRAYERS
FOR
HEALING

by John Gunstone

**To help you pray for others as well as
for yourself**

Prayers for home and hospital; Personal prayers;
Corporate prayers; Prayers with responses;
Thanksgivings; Praying the Psalms; Praying with
the Scriptures; Ministry of reconciliation;
Sacramental ministry; A service of prayer for
healing; Guide to spontaneous prayer.

A practical and pastoral handbook.

ISBN 0 946616 35 3

LORD
HEAL ME

by John Gunstone

Prayers of compassion, understanding and faith for personal use

Here are prayers for every kind of illness and disablement, for emotional disorders as well as organic ailments. Simple morning and evening devotions for a patient, plus a selection of prayers for healing by Christians past and present.

ISBN 0 946616 40 X